S0-AAI-427

THE BEST IN TENT CAMPING:

FLORIDA

*A Guide for Campers Who Hate RVs, Concrete Slabs, and
Loud Portable Stereos*

THE BEST IN TENT CAMPING:

FLORIDA

---

*A Guide for Campers Who Hate RVs, Concrete Slabs, and
Loud Portable Stereos*

Johnny Molloy

Menasha
Ridge
Press, Inc.

Copyright © 1998 by Johnny Molloy
All rights reserved
Printed in the United States of America
Published by Menasha Ridge Press
First edition, first printing

Library of Congress Cataloging-in-Publication Data

Molloy, Johnny, 1961–
    The best in tent camping : Florida: a guide for campers who hate RVs,
concrete slabs, and loud portable stereos /
    Johnny Molloy.—1st ed.
      p.   cm.
    Includes bibliographical references (p. 169)
    ISBN 0-89732-273-8
    1. Camp sites, facilities, etc.—Florida—Guidebooks.   2. Camping—
Florida—Guidebooks. 3. Florida—Guidebooks.   I. Title.
GV191.42.F6M65   1998
917.5904'63—dc21

                                                              98-9715
                                                                 CIP

Cover design by Grant Tatum
Cover photo by Dennis Coello
Maps by Brian Taylor

Menasha Ridge Press
P.O. Box 43059
Birmingham, Alabama 35243

CONTENTS

Central Florida

South Florida

Appendices

MAP LEGEND

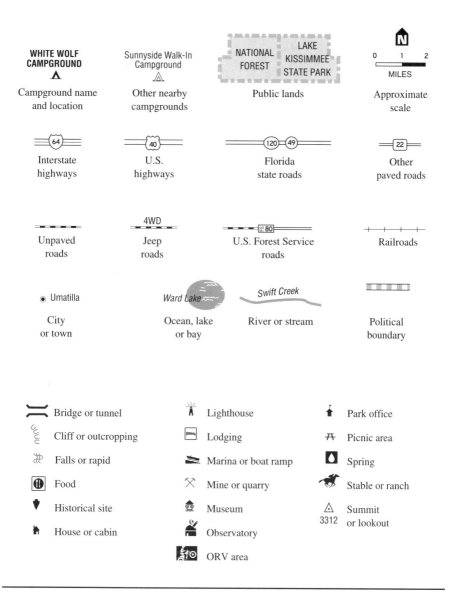

WHITE WOLF CAMPGROUND

Campground name and location

Sunnyside Walk-In Campground

Other nearby campgrounds

NATIONAL FOREST / LAKE KISSIMMEE STATE PARK

Public lands

0   1   2
MILES

Approximate scale

64
Interstate highways

40
U.S. highways

120 49
Florida state roads

22
Other paved roads

Unpaved roads

4WD
Jeep roads

80
U.S. Forest Service roads

Railroads

⊙ Umatilla
City or town

Ward Lake
Ocean, lake or bay

Swift Creek
River or stream

Political boundary

Bridge or tunnel

Cliff or outcropping

Falls or rapid

Food

Historical site

House or cabin

Lighthouse

Lodging

Marina or boat ramp

Mine or quarry

Museum

Observatory

ORV area

Park office

Picnic area

Spring

Stable or ranch

3312 Summit or lookout

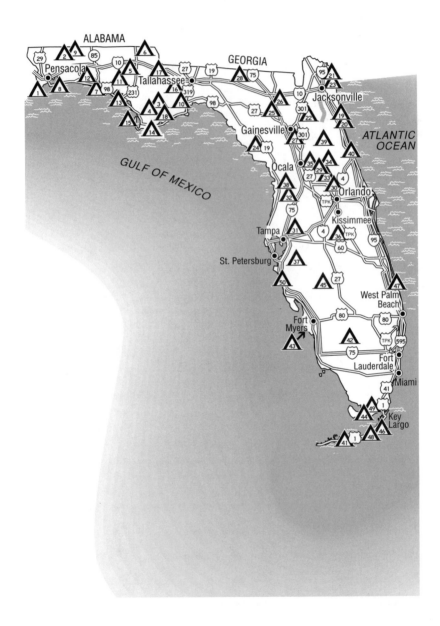

THE PANHANDLE

1. Big Lagoon
2. Blackwater River
3. Camel Lake
4. Dead Lakes
5. Falling Waters
6. Florida Caverns
7. Grayton Beach
8. Gulf Islands
9. Karick Lake South
10. Ochlockonee River
11. Pine Log
12. Rocky Bayou
13. St. Andrews
14. St. George Island
15. St. Joseph Peninsula
16. Silver Lake
17. Torreya
18. Wright Lake

NORTH FLORIDA

19. Anastasia
20. Faver-Dykes
21. Fort Clinch
22. Gold Head Branch
23. Little Talbot Island
24. Manatee Springs
25. O'Leno
26. Ocean Pond
27. Paynes Prairie
28. Suwannee River

CENTRAL FLORIDA

29. Alexander Springs
30. Blue Spring
31. Hillsborough River
32. Hog Island
33. Hontoon Island
34. Juniper Springs
35. Lake Eaton
36. Lake Kissimmee
37. Little Manatee River
38. Mutual Mine
39. Salt Springs
40. Tomoka

SOUTH FLORIDA

41. Bahia Honda
42. Bear Island
43. Cayo Costa
44. Flamingo
45. Highlands Hammock
46. John Pennekamp
47. Jonathan Dickinson
48. Long Key
49. Long Pine Key
50. Oscar Scherer

This book is for Hunt Cochrane,
a fair canoer, a good camper, a better backpacker,
and a great friend.

ACKNOWLEDGMENTS

Writing this book was an adventure in itself. Along the way I met old friends and new. I learned a lot and received help from many people. Thanks to Skip Krassa, the Pole from Baltimore; Eddie Duval, Commissioner City of Miami; J. L. Plummer; Lisa Daniel; Irv Edwards; Anthony Lauria; Advanced Systems of Sebring; Ranger Julie Watson; Barbara and Eve of Cayo Costa; Roger Chubin; George Drinnon; Nelle Molloy; Maggie Bryars; Brian Babb; Meredith Morris-Babb; and Debbie and Tom Lauria.

I thank all the Florida state park and state forest employees who helped me out, as well as all other public servants who endured my endless questions.

Finally, a special thanks goes to Hunt Cochrane, Kim Breasseale, David Zaczyk, and all the campers who love wild Florida as much as I do.

THE BEST IN TENT CAMPING:

FLORIDA

A Guide for Campers Who Hate RVs, Concrete Slabs, and Loud Portable Stereos

PREFACE

Florida is well known as a vacation getaway for those weary of northern winters, those seeking a tropical atmosphere and oceanside ambience. A century ago, the Sunshine State was a sleepy, agricultural land of orange groves and cattle ranches. Since then, we have seen the rise of the urban landscape, as winter visitors decided to make Florida their permanent home. Vacationers continue to come, enjoying the cities as much as the climate. Modern times have seen the development of man-made attractions that have become destinations in their own right.

Florida continues to grow. Fortunately for us, state and federal governments have intervened to preserve the natural beauty of Florida, the same beauty encountered by Ponce de Leon's men as they searched for the fountain of youth. They didn't realize it at the time, but the Spaniards were traversing some of the most lush and unique landscapes in what would later become the United States.

Today, we can still see what Ponce de Leon saw: rolling sand hills of the central ridge, sugar-white beaches of the Gulf Coast, vast mangrove stands of the Everglades, incredible rivers of all lengths and varieties, pine flatwoods whose needles perfume the air. This is what the Division of State Parks likes to call "the real Florida."

After you have explored some of this state's natural preserves, new images of Florida will emerge: not only Miami's South Beach but also the blue water of the Keys, not only Disney World but Hontoon Island as well, not only Cape Canaveral but the federal batteries at Fort Clinch too. Your revised picture of Florida will include natural preserves, the human history of Florida: the original cowboys, known as "crackers" in a living history demonstration at Lake Kissimmee; the Timucuan Indian artifacts at Tomoka; a pioneer homestead at Highlands Hammock; and more.

A fine tent-camping experience will enhance your exploration of Florida. I combed the state in search of the best outdoors combination: fine tent camping coupled with interesting scenic locales. My problem was picking only the 50 best campgrounds. Whether you are a native Floridian in search of new territory or an out-of-state vacationer, this book will help you unlock the secrets to the real, natural Florida.

—*Johnny Molloy*

INTRODUCTION

A Word about This Book and Florida Camping

Florida is a tent camper's paradise. From the northwestern Panhandle to the Everglades, there are natural areas, still wild, that have been developed enough to include quality campgrounds. So, you can camp in an attractive setting and have plenty of nature nearby to enjoy. And with the focus on tourism in the state, you're never more than a couple hours' drive from attractions designed for the out-of-towner.

Tent-camping opportunities vary with the change of season in Florida. Yes, there is a degree of seasonality in Florida, a seasonality that is more noticeable the farther north you are. Tallahassee can get downright cold in January. Also, the change of seasons north of the state line will affect your tent-camping experience south of it. In winter, "snowbirds" descend from Canada and the northern states, occupying the campgrounds in south and central Florida. In summer, many of these same campgrounds become deserted.

Many snowbirds travel in RVs. Usually the RVs and tents are separated; however, in some campgrounds, they are not. Some of the best campgrounds mix RVs and tent campers; these campgrounds had other qualities too good to eliminate them from this book for that reason alone. That's just the way of the camping world in some parts of Florida. Don't let it bother you.

As you move north, there are campgrounds, especially oceanside ones, that get a modicum of year-round traffic. Winter can bring a solitude that is not experienced at other times of the year at certain Panhandle campgrounds. So, when tent camping in Florida, take the time of year into account when picking your getaway. To help with your planning, I have included in the each campground description my recommendation for the best time of year to camp there.

A few words of advice: Call ahead and ask for a park brochure, map, or other information to help you plan your trip. Get reservations where applicable, especially in the Keys. Ask questions. Ask more questions. The more questions you ask, the fewer surprises you'll get. There are others times, however, when you'll grab your gear and this book, hop in the car, and just wing it. This can be an adventure in its own right.

In Florida, you must plan for the probability of bugs. Mosquitoes and no-see-ums can plot to ruin a camping trip. Don't let them do it. Bring repellent, a tent with fine mesh netting, and a good attitude.

The rating system

Included in this book is a rating system for Florida's 50 best campgrounds. Certain campground attributes—beauty, privacy, spaciousness, quiet, security, and cleanliness/upkeep—are ranked using a star system. Five stars are ideal and one star is acceptable. This way you can find the campground that has the attributes you desire.

Beauty

In the best campgrounds, the fluid shapes of nature—flora, water, land, and sky—have melded to create locales that seem to have been made for tent camping. The best sites are so attractive you may be tempted not to leave your outdoor home. A little site work is OK to make the scenic area camper-friendly, but too many reminders of civilization eliminated many a campground from inclusion in this book.

Site privacy

A little understory goes a long way in making you feel comfortable once you've picked your site for the night. There is a trend of planting natural borders between campsites if the borders don't already exist. With some trees or brush to define the sites, each camper has his or her own personal space. You can go about the pleasures of tent camping without keeping up with the Joneses at the next site over—or them with you.

Site spaciousness

This attribute can be very important depending on how much of a gearhead you are and the size of your group. Campers with family-style tents need a large, flat spot on which to pitch their tent and still get to the ice chest to prepare foods, all the while not getting burned near the fire ring. Gearheads need adequate space to show off all of their stuff to the neighbors strolling by. I just want enough room to keep my bedroom, kitchen, and den separate.

Quiet

Nature's symphony—waves lapping against the shore, singing birds, wind rushing through the pines, and thunderstorms passing in the night—is the kind of noise tent campers associate with being in Florida. In concert, they camouflage the sounds you don't want to hear: autos coming and going, loud neighbors, and the like.

Security

Campground security is relative. A remote campground with no civilization nearby is relatively safe, but don't tempt potential thieves by leaving your valuables out for all to see. Use common sense and go with your instincts. Campground hosts are wonderful to have around, and state parks with locked gates at night are ideal for security. Get to know your neighbors and develop a buddy system to watch each other's belongings whenever possible.

Cleanliness/upkeep

I'm a stickler for this one. Nothing will sabotage a scenic campground like trash. Most of the campgrounds in this book are clean. More rustic camp-grounds, my favorites, usually receive less maintenance. Busy weekends and holidays will show their effects. But don't let a little litter spoil your good time. Help clean up and think of it as doing your part for our natural envi-ronment.

FLORIDA
PANHANDLE

BIG LAGOON CAMPGROUND

Pensacola

L ocated on the Intercoastal Waterway, Big Lagoon is Florida's most westerly recreation area. The water-dominated park has oceanside fishing, boating, hiking, and swimming. Nearby Perdido Key Recreation Area features a white-sand Gulf beach. Big Lagoon's campground has good, varied sites to suit any camper's desires. Look over the campground before you pick a site or you'll drive by a campsite that you wish you could have had.

Big Lagoon Campground was built on an ancient, wooded sand dune, which accounts for the varied campsites you find there today A very long and narrow loop road runs along either low side of the dune. This setup makes for a rolling campground with vertical relief. Differing degrees of forest cover make for sunny, open campsites and hidden, wooded campsites.

Tall slash pines tower above the campground. But the more prevalent pine is the low-slung sand pine that favors sandy coastal regions like Big Lagoon. Live oaks grow about, but they don't reach the heights seen farther inland. Plants like dune rosemary combine with wax myrtle, winged sumac, and palmetto to form thick campsite buffers that shield you from your neighbor.

The first two-thirds of the campground have electrical hookups. The campsites on the right-hand side of the loop are higher

CAMPGROUND RATINGS

Beauty:	★★★★
Site privacy:	★★★★
Site spaciousness:	★★★★
Quiet:	★★★
Security:	★★★★★
Cleanliness/upkeep:	★★★★

An attractive, quality campground enhances watery Big Lagoon State Recreation Area.

and have less-dense wood-lands. The other side of the loop backs against a marsh and has campsites cut into moist woods. Still other sites are cut into the dune and have wooden walls to hold back the sand.

The back of the campground has 25 nonelectric campsites that are best suited for tent campers. There are sites on both sides of the loop. Fragile buffer vegetation is protected by quaint wooden fences that separate some of the camp-sites. This area is the highest in the campground and has many appealing sites. Adequate space and privacy can be found at nearly every site.

There are three clean and modern comfort stations that serve the campground. Campground hosts and on-site rangers make this a very safe place to camp.

Park recreation is just a walk away. Two nature trails leave the campground via boardwalks and connect to the waters of the Intercoastal Waterway. There are two swimming areas: East Beach and West Beach. Neat, wooden picnic pavilions offer refuge from the sun during times of play in the water. East Beach has an observation tower overlooking the surrounding Gulf beaches and waters. Quality saltwater fishing for sea trout and flounder is available. Boaters have a boat ramp to launch their craft. Hungry campers can even go crabbing in Big Lagoon.

All these nature trails connect to make nearly all park areas accessible. The Yaupon Trail meanders right along the Gulf. The Grand Lagoon Trail connects East Beach to West Beach and has a side trail to Big Lagoon itself. The 3.5-mile Cookie Trail is a one-way trek that starts near the park entrance station. It passes through open pine woods and nearly impenetrable thickets gnarled from the salt and wind of the maritime weather.

It is about a 15-minute drive to Perdido Key from Big Lagoon. Perdido Key State Recreation Area is a 247-acre enclave of protected Gulf coast. There are over 1.4 miles of beach to enjoy. Clear waters meld into white-sand beaches which meld into rolling sand dunes covered with sea oats. Several boardwalks crisscross the environment, making for safe passage across the fragile sand dunes. To access Perdido Key, turn left out of Big Lagoon and then take your next left onto State Road 292; follow it a short distance to the state recreation area.

Big Lagoon was a pleasant surprise for me. I really liked the unusual campground stretched along the ancient sand dune. The park recreation and that of nearby Perdido Key avail any tent camper ample reason to give Big Lagoon a try.

To get there from Pensacola, take U.S. 98 west from Navy Boulevard for 6 miles to SR 293 (Bauer Road). Turn left on SR 293 and head south for 5 miles to dead end at Big Lagoon State Recreation Area.

KEY INFORMATION

Big Lagoon Campground
12301 Gulf Beach Highway
Pensacola, FL 32507

Operated by: Florida State Parks

Information: (904) 492-1595

Open: Year-round

Individual sites: 48

Each site has: Picnic table, fire ring, water

Site assignment: Assigned by ranger unless specific site asked for

Registration: By phone or at park entrance booth

Facilities: Hot showers, flush toilets, pay phone

Parking: At campsites only

Fee: $8 per night; $2 electricity fee

Elevation: Sea level

Restrictions

Pets—Prohibited

Fires—In fire rings only

Alcoholic beverages—Prohibited

Vehicles—None

Other—14-day stay limit

BLACKWATER RIVER CAMPGROUND

Milton

CAMPGROUND RATINGS

Beauty:	★★★★
Site privacy:	★★★
Site spaciousness:	★★★
Quiet:	★★★★
Security:	★★★★★
Cleanliness/upkeep:	★★★★

Florida's finest canoe-touring river is the namesake and centerpiece of this serene state park.

The Blackwater River enjoys a reputation as the cleanest river in the state of Florida. Most of its upper drainage flows through protected forest lands. The clear waters have a reddish tint from tree tannin. The river bottom is sugar-white sand. This sand builds to form sandbars on river bends. These sandbars make great swimming, picnicking, and overnight camping spots for river runners. Most canoeists end their trips at Blackwater River State Park, which makes it a great base camp to canoe not only the Blackwater but also three other fantastic waters nearby: Sweetwater, Juniper, and Coldwater Creeks. Many outfitters serve the locality, which makes an outing convenient and easy, whether you have your own canoe or not.

The campground is fairly scenic in its own right. Heavily wooded, with a dense growth of campsite buffers, the camping area is split into two loops. The heady aroma of longleaf pine, the predominant tree, filters through the campground. Oak, maple, and a few hardwoods are scattered about. The close proximity to the Blackwater brings some riverine flora to the area.

The right-hand loop has 15 campsites. Dense vegetation forms ideal campsite buffers for tent campers. This is the shadier of the two loops and is closer to the river. The campsites are smaller here than on the other loop yet have adequate space.

Generally, a little sacrificed space is the price you pay for increased privacy.

The left-hand loop has 15 campsites as well. Having two loops disperses campers and increases the sense of serenity here at Blackwater. The campsites here are bigger and more open than those on the right-hand loop. The larger size of the campsites attracts some RVs to this particular loop.

Be careful of which campsite you pick if it looks like rain— some of these sites are in low-lying areas and look vulnerable

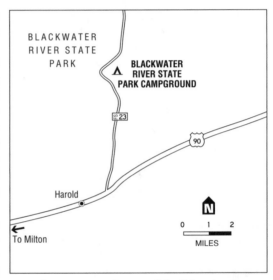

to ponding of water. Ponding water under your tent is a terrible thing to stir you from your slumber.

The canoeing season in the Blackwater heats up in May and lasts through September. This is when the campground gets busy, too. The cooler months are very quiet, save for travelers looking for an overnight stopping place. Reservations aren't made here, but an early weekend arrival will most likely land a pleasant campsite.

You don't have to canoe the Blackwater to enjoy the cool water and white sand. A boardwalk leads from the river parking area to covered picnic shelters and the river. Here you can sunbathe and swim. Check out the Florida-record Atlantic white cedar tree along the boardwalk.

Hikers have two trails on which to stretch their legs. A short nature trail leaves the campground and leads to the river. The trail loops a small pond that was once the course of the shallow Blackwater. On the other side of the river is the 1-mile Chain of Lakes Trail. It follows the river and then meanders through low-lying cypress swamps and small lakes.

But the main activity at Blackwater is canoeing. Several outfitters in the area will be glad to serve you. On my trips down local rivers, I have used Adventures Unlimited. The number is (800) 239-6864. The staff will rent canoes or provide shuttle service for those who bring their own watercraft.

Why canoe the Blackwater? Cedar trees lining the riverbanks. Cypress, oak, and maple trees swaying in the breeze. Pine trees on the higher ground. Swift-moving waters sweeping around bends, passing huge white sandbars that beckon you to wiggle your toes in the sand. The relaxation of just floating down the river. A riverbank picnic. Sun on your face. Clean, natural water that you feel comfortable swimming in.

Other smaller streams in the area exhibit these same qualities. I like Coldwater Creek. It is small, shallow, and fast, supposedly the fastest water in the area. Fallen trees on bends keep canoeists on their toes. Ample sandbars allow for frequent stops.

You can paddle two creeks on the Sweetwater/Juniper run. These are even smaller than Coldwater. Start on the Sweetwater to its confluence with the Juniper and keep floating down the Juniper. Other runs solely on the Juniper are rewarding, too. Keep an eye downriver as logs and submerged obstructions can come up quickly on these swift streams.

This water-oriented park has a fine campground. It's a pleasant stay even if you are not a paddler. The park section of the Blackwater is accessible for foot travelers. So, one way or another, get in the water at Blackwater River State Park.

KEY INFORMATION

**Blackwater River Campground
Route 1, Box 57-C
Holt, FL 32564**

Operated by: Florida State Parks

Information: (904) 983-5363

Open: Year-round

Individual sites: 30

Each site has: Picnic table, fire ring, water, electricity

Site assignment: First come, first served; no reservations

Registration: At Ranger Station

Facilities: Hot showers, flush toilets, pay phone

Parking: At campsites only

Fee: $8 per night; $2 electricity fee

Elevation: 30 feet

Restrictions

Pets—Prohibited

Fires—In fire rings only

Alcoholic beverages—Prohibited

Vehicles—None

Other—14-day stay limit

To get there from Milton, drive east on U.S. 90 for 11 miles to the tiny town of Harold. Turn left on FS 23, which will have a sign indicating it is the route to Blackwater River State Park. Follow FS 23 for 3 miles to Blackwater River State Park.

CAMEL LAKE CAMPGROUND

Bristol

Small, quiet, and scenic. Camel Lake Campground is being revamped by the Forest Service, but the natural beauty cannot be improved upon—an open forest with an understory of grass that turns to brooding cypress trees covered in Spanish moss by the lake. The body of water is the focal point of the recreation area. Bicyclers and hikers will be glad to know that the Florida National Scenic Trail and a few other paths make overland recreation possible, too.

As it stands, there are only six campsites. There once were 11, and the figure may change again with time, but the overall number of campsites will remain small. It couldn't be any other way at this off-the-beaten-path campground.

The campground is located on a gentle slope leading to Camel Lake. A short dirt road connects the camping area with the day use area. Camel Lake Campground is mostly open but is punctuated by pine trees and turkey oaks. A sporadic understory of palmetto breaks up the camping area. The first three sites are located on a grassy lawn, surrounded on three sides by woods. Campsites 1 and 3 are set away from the road against the woodland. Campsite 2 is close to the road beneath a pine tree.

The other three campsites are on the downside of the road. They are closer to the lake, in a grassy lawn of their own. Campsites 4 and 5 are near the camp-

CAMPGROUND RATINGS

Beauty:	★★★
Site privacy:	★★
Site spaciousness:	★★★★★
Quiet:	★★★★
Security:	★★★
Cleanliness/upkeep:	★★★★

Camel Lake is the Apalachicola National Forest's quiet recreation retreat.

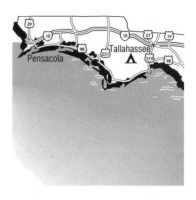

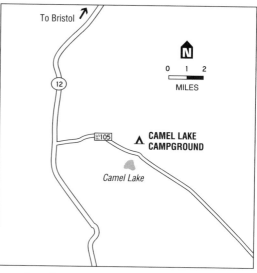

ground road. The final site is set against a woodland where the Camel Lake Loop Trail comes in.

The campground bathhouse is about 50 yards away in the day use area. It has flush toilets for each sex. This area used to be part of the campground and may be again in the future. A grassy lawn overlooks the lake and is backed by a denser forest than the campground. A cold-water shower is out in the open in the day use area; wear your trunks or swimsuit if you shower here.

Spring-fed Camel Lake attracts anglers from all around. Big bass have been pulled out of these waters. Bream and catfish are here, too. Launch your boat at the nearby boat ramp. Directly below the day use area is a large, grassy lawn that leads down to a swimming beach. The swimming area is ringed off for children's safety.

The backbone of Florida's hiking, the Florida National Scenic Trail passes right by Camel Lake. Follow the blue blazes on the trees from the recreation area entrance and go a few hundred feet to intersect the orange-blazed trail. You can go either north or south on this trail. The southern route travels through varied environments from dry, sandhill country to junglelike areas near streams. The northern route swings by Memery Island to end at County Road 12. Arrange for a shuttle to pick you up.

The Camel Lake Loop Trail starts at the boat launch. The numbered footpath circles Camel Lake and smaller Camel Pond. If you follow the numbers in their entirety, the loop trip is 1.8 miles. If you bypass Camel Pond and only circle Camel Lake, the trip is 1.2 miles. Camel Pond has a few fish in it, too. The Camel Lake Interpretive Trail starts just across the road from the campground entrance. Signs tell you all about this Florida Panhandle forest on the 1-mile loop.

This is about as small as campgrounds come. A campground host mans the front gate, making for a safer campground. The day use area at Camel Lake can be busy on summer weekends, but with only six campsites, the campground can't get too crowded. Set up your tent and get to know your fellow campers.

To get there from Bristol, take CR 12 south for about 11 miles. Turn left on FS 105 and drive 2 miles. Camel Lake Campground will be on your right.

Camel Lake Campground
State Highway 20
P.O. Box 579
Bristol, FL 32321

Operated by: U.S. Forest Service

Information: (904) 643-2282

Open: Year-round

Individual sites: 6

Each site has: Picnic table, fire ring

Site assignment: First come, first served; no reservations

Registration: Self-registration on site

Facilities: Cold shower, flush toilets, water spigots

Parking: At campsites only

Fee: $4 per night

Elevation: 55 feet

Restrictions

Pets—On 6-foot leash only

Fires—In fire rings only

Alcoholic beverages—Prohibited

Vehicles—None

Other—14-day stay limit

FLORIDA PANHANDLE

DEAD LAKES CAMPGROUND

Wewahitchka

U pon arriving at Dead Lakes State Recreation Area, it took me a while to locate the park ranger. When I found him, we talked about the park. Our conversation lasted over two hours. You see, the ranger at Dead Lakes is always glad to see visitors. Dead Lakes is *very* quiet. It's not that the place is unappealing—it's just near enough to the beach that most campers just pass it by. The name doesn't exactly draw you in either. But the solitude you find here happens to be Dead Lakes' greatest asset.

Weeks go by and no one camps in the campground. This small park—83 acres—sees a fair share of day visitors. They are mostly locals doing a little fishing in the Dead Lakes. Granted, this isn't a place to spend two weeks, but the park makes an ideal overnighting place on the way to the Gulf beaches or a place where you can have the whole campground to yourself. No hustle and bustle here. None whatsoever.

The small campground it is located under a stand of tall longleaf pines. An old, sand road makes a loop through the woods. At the beginning of the loop are three campsites that have the most bushes in the campground. But campsite privacy is not relevant here. Chances are you'll have the entire campground to yourself. The understory of grass and pinecones in the campsite parking spots stands testimony to the underuse of this little-known campground.

CAMPGROUND RATINGS

Beauty: ★★★
Site privacy: ★★★★★
Site spaciousness: ★★★★
Quiet: ★★★★★
Security: ★★★★
Cleanliness/upkeep: ★★★★

Dead Lakes offers the most solitude of any campground rated in this book.

Beyond the three sites is the beginning of ten campsites located on the inside of the loop. All these sites have electricity and more sand than grass for an understory. If you brought your TV and want to hook it up, stay in one of these sites. You'll also be closer to the immaculate comfort station in the loop's center. It has hot showers and flush toilets and is guaranteed to be unoccupied.

As the loop continues around, other large sites are on the outside of the loop and are on the highest land in the camp-

ground. These sites are fine as well. Just take your time; nobody will be driving up to steal your coveted campsite.

If you've been driving a bit, there is about a mile's worth of nature trails to walk and stretch your legs. They start right near the campground and pass by some old ponds that were once used to hold fish for a nearby hatchery.

Of course, the primary waters are the Dead Lakes themselves, which is really one lake. Dead Lakes—what a name! This place came to be when sandbars formed where the Chipola River entered the Apalachicola River. This backed the water up and flooded the Chipola, creating five wide spots in the river. This flooding killed a vast number of trees in the new lake, which thereafter became known as the Dead Lakes.

Mankind meddled with the relationship between the Chipola and Apalachicola, but today things are fine with the lake. Dead Lakes offers some seriously good bass fishing. A boat ramp is located at the park. You can use a canoe or powerboat to angle for bream and crappie, as well as bass. A quality canoe run on the Chipola ends at the Dead Lakes. Outfitters are located near Marianna.

I enjoyed my visit to the park. A warm wind blew through the spring day as I ate lunch in the picnic area near the campground. The campground was my own. Actually the whole park was my own. It was a bit sweaty walking the nature trails, but the wind was too strong to canoe the lake.

When you come to Dead Lakes, don't expect to have other campers for company. Bring in all your own supplies, entertainment, and company. But before you leave, be sure to find the ranger. He enjoys a little company every now and then.

To get there from Wewahitchka, drive north on FL 71 for 2 miles. Turn right and dead-end into Dead Lakes State Recreation Area.

KEY INFORMATION

**Dead Lakes Campground
P.O. Box 989
Wewahitchka, FL 32465**

Operated by: Florida State Parks

Information: (904) 639-2702

Open: Year-round

Individual sites: 10 electric, 10 nonelectric

Each site has: Picnic table, fire ring

Site assignment: First come, first served; no reservations

Registration: Ranger will come by and register you

Facilities: Hot showers, flush toilets, water spigots

Parking: At campsites only

Fee: $8 per night; $2 electricity fee

Elevation: 40 feet

Restrictions

Pets—Prohibited

Fires—In fire rings only

Alcoholic beverages—Prohibited

Vehicles—None

FLORIDA PANHANDLE

FALLING WATERS CAMPGROUND
Chipley

I was surprised upon seeing this 155-acre state recreation area. The small size had me wondering just how good it could be. It was better than expected. Granted, the small dimension limits how much you can do and how long you will want to stay, but if you have a night and are in the area, don't pass it by. The hilltop campground is long on appeal and short on crowds. The natural features of the park are worth an afternoon of your time.

The Pine Ridge Camping Area sits at the park's high point. It's 250 feet in elevation, lofty country by Florida standards. Top the hill and enter a grove of longleaf and slash pine. The U-shaped campground road slowly curves to the left and descends a mild slope. Vertical relief in Florida campgrounds is unusual and adds to the scenic beauty of this particular one.

Four of the first five campsites are pull-through. This spells RV; but don't worry, there probably won't be more than one RV in the entire campground. Actually, you'll be hard pressed for neighbors, whether they be tent campers or RVers. The ranger told me Falling Waters averaged two or three campers per night at the 24-unit campground. It fills up two weekends per year: Memorial Day and Labor Day.

Beyond the pull-through sites starts a string of ten campsites; these sites are the park's best. Between tall pines are stretches of grass strewn with pine needles and pep-

CAMPGROUND RATINGS

Beauty: ★★★★
Site privacy: ★★★
Site spaciousness: ★★★★★
Quiet: ★★★★
Security: ★★★★★
Cleanliness/upkeep: ★★★★★

This little park with the pretty hilltop campground makes for a pleasant one-night stopover.

pered with pinecones. A few bushes break up the area. It just has the look that makes you want to run through it. These prime campsites are on both sides of the paved road.

Pass a couple of sites at the low point of the campground and the road starts to climb again. Here are two more pull-through sites. But there are also three pull-in sites at the back of a small turnaround that are very appealing.

There are a few wax myrtles, dogwoods, and turkey oaks about the campground; how-

ever, they provide little in the way of campsite privacy. Yet, here at Falling Waters, privacy is a nonissue because you will most likely be camping 100 feet or more from any other campers. And speaking of room, the campsites offer the maximum in site spaciousness.

The main attraction of the park is also an unusual Florida feature—a waterfall. The Falling Water Sink is a designated Florida Natural Feature. Though this area has hills, to get a 67-foot fall requires a hole—a sinkhole. The waterfall is created by a small creek flowing into a cylindrical hole. Take the Sinks Trail to the waterfall. As you descend the walkway to the falls, the air around you cools significantly. The waterfall truly is attractive.

Two other neat nature trails spur off the Sinks Trail. The Wiregrass Trail passes through pine woodland past an old, oil well drill site. This was one of the first oil drilling locations in the Sunshine State. This area also saw a grist mill and even a little moonshining back in the olden days.

The Sinkhole Trail rides a boardwalk up, down, and around more sinkholes of varying sizes and depths. It's a good thing this trail has a handrail—previous hikers have probably fallen in. The Terrace Trail runs from the campground through an old pine plantation—watch for the rows of trees. This area was also the site of a plant nursery in the early 1900s. The trail ends at a two-acre lake with a roped-off swimming area and a small beach.

As you can see, Falling Waters State Recreation Area makes the most of its 155 acres. The land is rural nearby, resulting in a peaceful setting that makes for a great one-night stopover in a pretty little campground.

To get there from Chipley, take FL 77 south for 4 miles to SR 77-A. Turn left on SR 77-A and follow it for 1 mile. Falling Waters State Recreation Area will be dead ahead.

KEY INFORMATION

Falling Waters Campground
Route 5, Box 660
Chipley, FL 32428

Operated by: Florida State Parks

Information: (904) 638-6130

Open: Year-round

Individual sites: 24

Each site has: Picnic table, fire ring, water, electricity

Site assignment: First come, first served; no reservations

Registration: At Ranger Station

Facilities: Hot showers, flush toilets

Parking: At campsites only

Fee: $8 per night; $2 electricity fee

Elevation: 250 feet

Restrictions

Pets—Prohibited

Fires—In fire rings only

Alcoholic beverages—Prohibited

Vehicles—None

FLORIDA CAVERNS CAMPGROUND

Marianna

The name of this state park emphasizes the uniqueness of the underground feature here. Strange and fascinating rock formations characterize the cave, where a tour guide leads you safely past the many sights to see. There are also many above-ground reasons to come to Florida Caverns, including the Chipola River and the Blue Hole Camping Area.

Camping here is an eye-pleasing experience in the diversely wooded setting. Laurel oaks and pines form the nucleus of the trees, but smaller beech, southern magnolia, and dogwood make for a varied setting in which to pitch your tent. Smaller trees and bushes allow for plenty of site privacy and create the impression that the campground was integrated into the forest rather than the other way around.

Blue Hole Camping Area is formed by a large, oval loop. The campground is split into four distinct sections, each containing eight campsites. A low-lying cypress swamp and Carters Mill Branch nearly encircle the campground with water, but the camping area is high and dry.

Half the sites are on the inside of the loop. Generally, the larger sites are on the outside of the loop, where I personally prefer to camp. But all the campsites are roomy; some are just extra roomy. Having the campsites spaced in four different sections along the loop provides everyone with plenty of personal room.

CAMPGROUND RATINGS

Beauty: ★★★★
Site privacy: ★★★
Site spaciousness: ★★★★
Quiet: ★★★
Security: ★★★★★
Cleanliness/upkeep: ★★★★

This state park has attractions above and below the ground. The camping is above ground and a Panhandle favorite.

If you can find it in the dense forest, the center of the loop holds a large bathhouse with all the expected amenities of a state park. This campground can fill up on summer and holiday weekends. Fall is an excellent time to come—the deciduous hardwoods can put on quite a colorful show throughout the park. It is fairly quiet during the winter. Spring sees many canoeists floating the Chipola.

No matter the weather or the season, Florida Caverns is ready to be toured. These tours

are offered daily. Just drive to the Visitor Center and wait for the next tour to begin. They last 45 minutes and are $4 for adults and $2 for children. From the roof of the cave, stalactites descend to meet the stalagmites pyramiding from the floor, ever rising from the minerals dripping from the ceiling above.

As you look at the impressive formations, be aware that they are being formed at the nearly imperceptible rate of one cubic inch per hundred years. Some of the pathways are a tight squeeze, but this makes the tour fun. The cave ranges from 62° to 68° F year-round. I give the tour a hearty recommendation.

Before or after you tour the cave, I also suggest walking the nature trails that depart from the Visitor Center parking area. The Floodplain Trail passes a couple of caves of its own. The trail looks out over the Chipola River. Indians once lived here; you can see a small shelter once used as living quarters. The Beech-Magnolia Trail connects with the Floodplain Trail and they all add up to over a mile of informative walking.

Near the campground is the Blue Hole. It is a spring that has been developed into a swimming area. A nice, grassy lawn is ideal for sunbathing, and a roped-off swimming spot will keep you cool. A short path connects the campground to the Blue Hole.

Fishermen and canoeists will want to utilize the Chipola River. It makes a good float. In the park, the river once sank into the ground then rose several hundred feet away; loggers have cut a channel reconnecting the river. Canoes are for rent at the park. Outfitters are based in the area and will rent canoes and provide shuttle service for a trip. Visit the park office for information.

The Blue Hole Campground is a relaxing setting. Florida Caverns State Park offers above-ground, below-ground, and water recreation. Come on by and give it a chance.

To get there from downtown Marianna, take CR 166 (Jefferson Street) 3 miles north. Florida Caverns State Park will be on your left.

KEY INFORMATION

Florida Caverns Campground
3345 Caverns Road
Marianna, FL 32446

Operated by: Florida State Parks

Information: (904) 482-9598

Open: Year-round

Individual sites: 32

Each site has: Picnic table, fire ring, water, electricity

Site assignment: Assigned by ranger unless specific site asked for

Registration: By phone or at park entrance booth

Facilities: Hot showers, flush toilets, pay phone

Parking: At campsites only

Fee: $8 per night October to February, $12 per night March to September; $2 electricity fee

Elevation: 120 feet

Restrictions

Pets—Prohibited

Fires—In fire rings only

Alcoholic beverages—Prohibited

Vehicles—None

Other—14-day stay limit

FLORIDA PANHANDLE

GRAYTON BEACH CAMPGROUND

Fort Walton Beach

Simply put, if you are in the area, don't pass by Grayton Beach State Recreation Area. The campground is heavily vegetated in native flora and is just the right size. Grayton Beach itself is as fine as the grains of white sand from which it is made. If you like to relax on the beach and come back to a relaxing private campground, this is the place for you.

Though the campground is not directly on the beach, it is close enough to hear the surf crashing against the shoreline. Between the ocean and the campground is a thin strip of land and Western Lake. Western Lake is a body of water with a moderate sand beach of its own that pales in scenery only when compared with one of the best beaches in the country.

The loop road design is the only standard thing about Grayton Beach Campground. A crushed-shell road passes through a thick wood. Overhead is a scattering of slash pines. The forest is mostly low, the result of the effects of salt spray and wind. Scrub oaks are blown into twisted shapes amid dense thickets of yaupon holly and palmetto. A few palm trees and cedars complete the vegetative picture.

This low-slung woodland is so thick that a camper can hardly see his neighbor. This campground ranks with the highest in campsite privacy. The disadvantage of the low forest is a lack of shade during the

CAMPGROUND RATINGS

Beauty:	★★★★★
Site privacy:	★★★★★
Site spaciousness:	★★★
Quiet:	★★★★
Security:	★★★★★
Cleanliness/upkeep:	★★★★

This small, attractive, quiet campground complements one of America's best beaches.

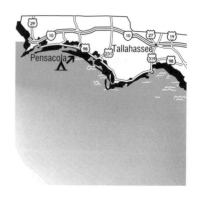

high-sun hours. But that won't matter because you will probably be at the beach anyway during that time.

Half the campsites are on the inside of the loop. In the interior loop, campsite privacy is not conceded. All of the campsites have enough room for the average camper. The first three campsites on the outside of the loop have no view. After that, the next eight campsites on the outside of the loop back up to Western Lake and offer a view of the lake, the salt marsh, and the

dunes on the far side of the lakeshore. I was lucky enough to get one of these sites. But if you aren't so lucky, little paths have been cut to access the small beach along Western Lake.

These paths, eight of them, are also used to access the obscured comfort station in the center of the campground loop. It is clean and modern. As the loop swings away from Western Lake, more pines appear overhead. There is less of an ocean breeze here. But these campsites are larger and would be more than acceptable on nearly everyone's list.

This relatively small park has a mile of world-class beach. Translucent, green waters meet sheer white sand backed by tall sand dunes covered in sea oats. This is the primary attraction at this state recreation area.

Being a nature trail fan, I walked the one here. It makes two loops. Odd sights on the trail are the tiny southern magnolias that merely reach bush size beacause of the ever-present wind and salt. The trail climbs dunes and parallels the shores of Western Lake. The nature trail then enters the pine flatwoods before returning to the beach. The foggy day made my beach walk seem even more mystical.

A boat ramp avails access to Western Lake. Fishermen can cast for both freshwater and saltwater species. Some people like to surf-fish from the shore. Canoes are for rent at a very reasonable rate; use them only on Western Lake.

But the main activity at Grayton Beach is relaxing. Take in some of that salt air and hang out on the beach. This is one place where you don't have to compromise your camping experience for the natural experience nearby.

To get there from Fort Walton Beach, drive east on U.S. 98 for 18 miles to CR 30-A. Head east on CR 30-A for 9 miles. Grayton Beach State Recreation Area will be on your right.

KEY INFORMATION

Grayton Beach Campground
357 Main Park Road
Santa Rosa Beach, FL 32549

Operated by: Florida State Parks

Information: (904) 231-4210

Open: Year-round

Individual sites: 37

Each site has: Picnic table, fire ring, water, electricity

Site assignment: Assigned by ranger unless specific site asked for

Registration: By phone or at park entrance booth

Facilities: Hot showers, flush toilets, pay phone

Parking: At campsites only

Fee: $8 per night November to February, $15 per night March to October; $2 electricity fee

Elevation: Sea level

Restrictions

Pets—Prohibited

Fires—In fire rings only

Alcoholic beverages—Prohibited

Vehicles—None

Other—14-day stay limit

GULF ISLANDS CAMPGROUND

Pensacola

Don't let the number of campsites at Gulf Islands National Seashore scare you away. The campground is big, but it has two loops that are for tent campers only. The blinding white beaches and fascinating Fort Pickens are worth putting up with lots of other campers.

The strangest part of the whole deal is getting used to the idea of camping and recreating at a former military installation. Fort Pickens was an active post until 1947. The campground consists of five paved loops with paved parking spots at each campsite. A pine overstory is mixed with some live oaks. The campground floor is a well-manicured grassy lawn. There are no bushes which means little or no campsite privacy. But the campground as a whole is immaculate.

Loop A has 43 campsites. It is situated all by itself off Fort Pickens Road. It accomodates all RVs. The other four loops spur off the main campground road. Go past the campground store; Loop C and Loop E are to your right. Between them they have 126 electric campsites with nothing but RVs and a stray tent camper. Loop E backs up to some old sand dunes near Pensacola Bay. The comfort stations are a little small for the number of campers they serve.

Up the way are the two loops for tent campers, Loops B and D. Loop B has 13 campsites. They are more spacious than the RV sites. Shade varies whether or not you

CAMPGROUND RATINGS

Beauty: ★★★★
Site privacy: ★
Site spaciousness: ★★★
Quiet: ★★★★
Security: ★★★★
Cleanliness/upkeep: ★★★★★

Miles of white beach, military history, and two tent-only loops await you at Gulf Islands National Seashore.

are under a live oak. The pines provide less shade. Remember, there is little campsite privacy here.

Loop D has 29 campsites. These sites are the quietest in the park. The cinderblock comfort station is a little on the older side but is kept clean by one of the many campground hosts that maintain the campground. Loop B also uses this comfort station. Two campsites in Loop D worth noting are 23 and 24. They are large and shady beneath some attractive live oaks.

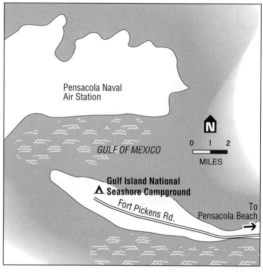

Langdon Beach is within walking distance of the campground. Cross Fort Pickens Road and take one of the two boardwalks. At Langdon Beach, miles of unspoiled sand and sea await you. This would be all condos and houses if the federal government hadn't stepped in to preserve this special piece of coastline. Two other boardwalks leave the campground and access Pensacola Bay. Between these areas there is enough sand to wear your legs out while beachcombing.

Woodland walkers can take the short Blackbird Marsh Nature Trail. It starts near Loop A. A bicycle trail also connects the campground to Langdon Beach. Bicyclers also pedal the roads of the park. It is 1 mile by foot on a section of the Florida Trail from the campground to Fort Pickens. The trail starts where Loops A and D meet.

I was fascinated by Fort Pickens. It is a conglomeration of old and new. You can see modern steel and concrete gun emplacements amid aged, brick structures. Go to the Visitor Center and pick up the self-guided tour of the fort. Geronimo was once kept prisoner here. Just one more oddity in an unusual place.

The fort was built here to defend the navy yard at Pensacola Bay. It was completed in 1834 and used for over 100 years. You'll see that the fort underwent many changes in the ensuing century. Building the fort was an undertaking in itself, using over 21 million bricks. Furthermore . . . oh, you'll get to learn the rest when you get here.

There are other military installations on this western tip of Santa Rosa Island. Battery Langdon is massive. In the Naval Live Oaks unit of the park, you'll find the main Visitor Center and several miles of nature trails that pass through ecosystems still intact in spite of coastal development that has ravaged much of the coast.

The beaches are worth it. The fort is worth it. The campground is pretty but large. Just try to overlook its size in order to look at all the good of the Gulf Islands National Seashore.

To get there from Pensacola, drive south on FL 399 for 7 miles to Pensacola Beach, passing over a toll bridge. In Pensacola Beach, turn right on Fort Pickens Road and dead-end at Gulf Islands National Seashore.

KEY INFORMATION

Gulf Islands Campground
1801 Gulf Breeze Parkway
Gulf Breeze, FL 32561

Operated by: National Park Service

Information: (904) 934–2621

Open: Year-round

Individual sites: 156 electric, 55 nonelectric

Each site has: Picnic table, fire grate, water

Site assignment: First come, first served; no reservations

Registration: At campground registration building

Facilities: Hot showers, flush toilets, camp store

Parking: At campsites and extra car parking

Fee: $20 per night electric, $15 per night nonelectric

Elevation: Sea level

Restrictions

Pets—On 6-foot leash only

Fires—In grills only

Alcoholic beverages—At campsites only

Vehicles—None

Other—14 days total from March to October; 30-day stay limit per calendar year

KARICK LAKE SOUTH CAMPGROUND

Munson

The Florida Division of Forestry has made a commitment to improve its campgrounds. The commitment shows at Karick Lake South. At one time, the facilities were minimal and rundown. Today, the lakeside campground matches the scenery of the longleaf/wire grass ecosystem in a rustic way that tenters will enjoy. Expect to get a lot of relaxing done at this peaceful camp.

The longleaf/wire grass ecosystem is the coastal plain's forest of longleaf pine trees and its ground cover known as wire grass. This woodland, dependent on fire lest it eventually evolve to hardwoods, once extended over 60 million acres in the South. Now, less than 3 million acres remain. The area around Karick Lake is part of the largest contiguous remnant of the longleaf/wire grass ecosystem.

Karick Lake South Campground is situated around an artificial yet scenic impoundment of 58 acres. The lake was created in 1965. Until recently, it looked like the campground had been left alone since that time. Now, the 15-campsite enclave has been overhauled. Level tent pads and running water have been installed at each site. Every site has been given a general face-lift.

As you descend toward the lake, the sandy road begins a wide loop, first passing a small but fully equipped comfort station, then a boat ramp and day use area

CAMPGROUND RATINGS

Beauty:	★★★
Site privacy:	★
Site spaciousness:	★★★★
Quiet:	★★★★
Security:	★★★
Cleanliness/upkeep:	★★★

Recently revamped, Karick Lake South offers the best tent camping in the Blackwater River State Forest.

with picnic tables. Then, as the road parallels Karick Lake, campsites lie on either side of the road. Overhead, a pretty grove of pines shade the campground, which is intemittently landscaped with azaleas.

The land gently slopes toward the lake. Eight of the campsites are directly waterside. The other seven campsites are across the road from the lake but offer scenic lake views, too, since they are higher on the hill. Before the renovations, campers would pitch their tents on the slope. But now the tent pads make for a level and eminently comfortable night's sleep. Grass remains the prominent campsite understory.

Across the lake you can see Karick Lake North Campground. It has electrical hookups and the RVs that often accompany plug-in camping. But on the south side, it's tent campers only. This is primarily a warm-weather, weekend use campground. Families and anglers find solace in the scenic area. It's really quiet on weekdays and the cooler months. You can practically have the campground to yourself in the off-season.

There is something to do for everyone—hiking, swimming, fishing, and relaxing. Life in the rural Panhandle moves quite a bit slower than the rest of the state. And that's a good thing.

Fishing is enjoyed by anglers of all ages. The state has managed these waters well. When the lake was flooded, much timber was left standing to provide fish habitat. The lake has been periodically drawn down to improve fish habitat by liming, to enhance the lake bed for increased spawning with oyster shells and to place brush bundles as additional fish attractors.

Largemouth bass are the primary game fish. Hook one of these on your line and get ready to fight. Sunshine bass are stocked here for sport fishing and research purposes. Bluegill and sunfish have made their way from the lake to the frying pan on many an occasion here. Catfish roam the lake bed. Make sure you have a Florida freshwater fishing license.

The master trail of the Blackwater River State Forest has a terminus here; it is the Jackson Red Ground Trail. Named after Andrew Jackson, the trail follows the route of an old, Indian trading path used by Jackson and his soldiers while exploring Florida in 1818. The "Red Ground" part of the name comes from the orange-red soil that the trail passes through on its 21-mile journey from Karick Lake to Red Rock Primitive Campground. As it winds through the longleaf/wire grass ecosystem, it also passes swamps, streams, and ideal bird and animal habitat.

One-way hikers can arrange for a shuttle ride that may include parts of the Wiregrass Trail, which connects Karick Lake to Hurricane Lake. A shorter, loop hike works its way around the shores of Karick Lake. After a hike, slip into the lake for a refreshing dip. Of course, you could just relax with a book and watch everyone else run around. Expect to take things slow and easy, because that's the way things are done in this part of the Panhandle.

To get there from Munson, drive east on FL 4 for 13 miles to Baker and CR 189. Turn left (north) onto CR 189 and follow it for 7 miles to the signed turn to Karick Lake. Follow the unnamed forest road for 1.2 miles to Karick Lake South Campground.

KEY INFORMATION

Karick Lake South Campground
11650 Munson Highway
Milton, FL 32570

Operated by: Florida Division of Forestry

Information: (904) 957-4201

Open: Year-round

Individual sites: 15

Each site has: Tent pad, picnic table, fire grate, water

Site assignment: First come, first served; no reservations

Registration: Self-registration on site

Facilities: Hot showers, flush toilets

Parking: At campsites only

Fee: $9 per night

Elevation: 150 feet

Restrictions

Pets—On leash only

Fires—In fire grates only

Alcoholic beverages—Prohibited

Vehicles—None

Other—14-day stay limit

FLORIDA PANHANDLE

OCHLOCKONEE RIVER CAMPGROUND

Sopchoppy

Virtually encircled by the St. Marks National Wildlife Refuge, Ochlockonee River State Park is an island within an island of the real Florida. The Ochlockonee River is brackish at this point since it's just a few miles from the ocean. The quiet campground is a great refuge for humans.

A packed-sand road enters the 30-site campground. Scrub live oak trees grow beneath stunted arms of longleaf pine, which stand guard over the campground. Smaller oak trees, palmetto, and other brush separate the campsites from one another. The canopy is open in spots, allowing for an airy and bright campground, yet still providing enough shade for every campsite. The landscaping in this campground is nearly perfect for the pine flatwoods in which it lies.

The first five campsites spur off from both sides of the loop. The next three sites are nonelectric. They jut out from a small parking area of their own. These sites are more private and roomier than the electric sites.

Next begins another stretch of electric sites. Some of these are entirely within the shade of oaks. Again, as the loop begins to circle back around, there are three more nonelectric sites with their own parking area. One path leads to the sites. The sites have an obscured view of the Ochlockonee River and offer the most privacy in the campground. These are the most desirable

CAMPGROUND RATINGS

Beauty:	★★★★
Site privacy:	★★★
Site spaciousness:	★★★
Quiet:	★★★★★
Security:	★★★★★
Cleanliness/upkeep:	★★★★★

Ochlockonee is for active campers who prefer to hear nothing but the sounds of nature at their campground.

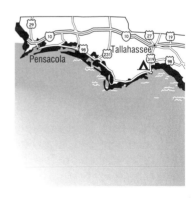

sites at this park, though nearly all the sites here are good.

Farther on, the electric campsites resume. One site on the inside of the loop is very open, looking over a grassy area. The final campsite on the inside of the loop is every bit as shady as the previous one was sunny. So you can choose your tree canopy here. The floor of the campsites is mostly grass with sand in spots.

A brand new bathhouse has been erected outside the east side of the loop. This campground is small enough to be reasonably accessible for all campers. The very center of the loop is grassy and has a play area for children.

Don't blink your eyes if you see white squirrels in the campground. There is a white subspecies of squirrel living in this park. There are a few other things here you might like to see, too, namely the water features. This park is practically encircled by the Dead River and the Ochlockonee River, both of which can be accessed by motorboat or canoe. Both rivers offer freshwater and saltwater fishing. Don't be surprised if you catch a largemouth bass one cast and a redfish on the next, then a bream, then a sea trout. The tides are very influential.

Various creeks, channels, and rivers wind through the grassy marsh around the park. These waterways make for fun exploration in a canoe, which can be rented in the park for a very reasonable rate. Obtain a free fishing map of the area at the park office before you explore.

Being surrounded by a wildlife refuge has its advantages. Ochlockonee is a wildlife viewer's paradise. Birders come from all over. Deer, bobcats, and even a bear or two have been known to call this park home. The Pine

Flatwoods Trail makes a loop through the center of the park. Beware of a sometimes wet section of the trail that crosses a marsh. A connector trail makes this loop accessible from the picnic area or the campground. Another trail runs along the Ochlockonee River behind the campground and ends at the boat ramp. The watery vistas are awesome.

There is a swimming area that is roped off near the outstanding picnic area. Have a meal beneath the shady oaks while looking over the water and marshlands beyond. An **L**-shaped dock extends out into the middle of the river. I watched a memorable sunrise there.

Other features nearby are Wakulla Springs and St. Marks Wildlife Refuge. Wakulla Springs is one of the world's largest. The water is incredibly clear. Take the glass-bottom boat tour and you can see the fossilized mastodon bones and the spring cavern 100 feet below! At St. Marks, stop by the Visitor Center and then head out to Pelican Point.

This is primarily a summertime campground. Weekends can fill, but Ochlockonee always has a relaxed pace. Winter may see a few visitors from the North. Once people come here, they realize what a quiet place it is. If you like to be serenaded to sleep by frogs and crickets instead of cars and trains, Ochlockonee River Campground is the place to come.

To get there from Sopchoppy, drive south on U.S. 319 for 4 miles. Ochlockonee River State Park will be on your left.

KEY INFORMATION

Ochlockonee River Campground
P.O. Box 5
Sopchoppy, FL 32358

Operated by: Florida State Parks

Information: (904) 962-2771

Open: Year-round

Individual sites: 24 electric, 6 nonelectric

Each site has: Picnic table, fire ring, water spigot

Site assignment: First come, first served; no reservations

Registration: Ranger will come by and register you

Facilities: Hot showers, flush toilets, pay phone, soda machine

Parking: At campsites only

Fee: $8 per night September to February, $10 per night March to August; $2 electricity fee

Elevation: 5 feet

Restrictions

Pets—Prohibited

Fires—In fire rings only

Alcoholic beverages—Prohibited

Vehicles—None

Other—14-day stay limit

PINE LOG CAMPGROUND

Panama City

Pine Log is an intimate 20-site lakeside campground as well as a primitive camping area with three campsites along Pine Log Creek. The vicinity is quiet and relaxed. If you want to avoid the busy beach campgrounds and you enjoy woodland camping, stay here. The budget-minded can stay at one of the primitive sites, use the main campground comfort station, and go to the public beaches of Panama City Beach.

You'll pass the reassuring site of the ranger's residence on Longleaf Road as you enter the Pine Log Recreation Area. The sandy lane swings right around East Lake. The campground begins with a series of eight campsites overlooking the lake. Seven of the eight sites are directly lakeside. Overhead is a canopy of longleaf pine. The understory is sorely lacking between campsites. However, the sites have adequate spaciousness and a good breeze rolling in off the lake.

The campground road veers away from the lake, but four more sites overlook the lake before the road turns completely away from the water. These campsites are especially roomy and aren't as coveted as the first lakeside sites. The ground cover here is more grass than sand.

The campground road turns to the left and there are campsites on both sides of the road, resting in a more heavily wooded area. These sites will be warmer in winter. If you like privacy, camp here because

CAMPGROUND RATINGS

Beauty: ★★★
Site privacy: ★★
Site spaciousness: ★★★
Quiet: ★★★★
Security: ★★★★★
Cleanliness/upkeep: ★★★★

Access Gulf beaches and the forest from this small, inland campground by a lake.

this area is obviously less frequented.

The campground as a whole
is never really busy. Weekdays
are always quiet. Spring and
summer weekends can see a
fair number of campers. Since
all the campsites have water
and electricity, some "snowbirds" will stop over during the
winter months. Summer is sporadic depending on the heat.

Back the other way on
Longleaf Road are the primitive
campsites. They are widely separated along a 1-mile stretch of
bumpy sand road passable by

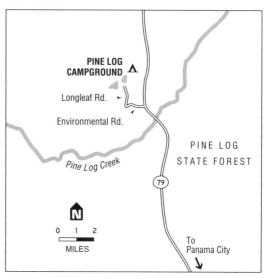

an ordinary passenger car. Each site is designated by a sign nailed to a tree. Beyond
the small parking spot is a short path that leads to the campsites. Each site has only
a tent spot and a fire ring. The coffee-colored and sand-bottomed Pine Log Creek
meanders by on the way to the Gulf. Each of these sites offers solitude not only
from the main campground but from each of the other primitive sites as well.

This makes a great place to stop if you are on the way to the Gulf or a great
inland site from which to make salty side trips. Yet, Pine Log has recreational
opportunities of its own. East Lake has a swimming area. Both East and West
lakes offer good freshwater fishing. Only hand-launched boats without power
motors are allowed on the lakes—canoes and the like. You can also canoe Pine
Log Creek. Put in near the primitive sites and take out at a boat ramp a few
miles down, as shown on the map at the campground.

Three trails start at the campground itself. The Campground Trail makes a
1.3-mile loop around both lakes and the campground. The 4-mile Edgar
"Dutch" Tiemann Nature Trail loops all the way down along Pine Log Creek
and back. An 8-mile section of the Florida National Scenic Trail runs through
this section of the forest.

On my trip I stayed at primitive camp-site 1. The pine forest descended toward the creek and became dominated by cypress trees near the camp. The day was overcast and cool as I started an early morning hike on the Tiemann Trail. I liked just walking right from my camp-site to the trail. I drove up to the main campground and showered. The after-noon cleared, so I made the half-hour drive down to the beach, returning to Pine Log in time to cook a campfire shish kebab before turning in for the night.

The quiet atmosphere of Pine Log lured me into an extra night's stay. I enjoyed the primitive campsite and the chance to enjoy both the saltwater and freshwater ecosystems. I recommend that you do the same.

To get there from Panama City, drive west on U.S. 98 for 10 miles to SR 79. Turn right on SR 79 and follow it for 12.6 miles to Environmental Road. Turn left on Environmental Road and follow it for 0.3 mile to Longleaf Road. Turn right on Longleaf Road and dead-end into the camp-ground in a short distance.

KEY INFORMATION

Pine Log Campground
715 West 15 Street
Panama City, FL 32401

Operated by: Florida Division of Forestry

Information: (904) 547-9071

Open: Year-round

Individual sites: 20 improved, 3 primitive

Each site has: Tent pad, picnic table, fire ring, water, elec-tricity

Site assignment: First come, first served; no reservations

Registration: Self-registration on site

Facilities: Hot showers, flush toilets

Parking: At campsites only

Fee: $12 per night improved, $4 per night primitive; $2 elec-tricity fee

Elevation: 20 feet

Restrictions

Pets—Prohibited

Fires—In fire rings only

Alcoholic beverages—Prohib-ited

Vehicles—None

Other—14-day stay limit

ROCKY BAYOU CAMPGROUND

Niceville

Overlooking an arm of Choctawahatchee Bay, Rocky Bayou has a nice waterfront campground with both land and water-oriented recreational opportunities. It is one of Florida's smaller state parks, so don't plan on an extended stay unless you just want to curl up with a good book at a quiet campground. Rocky Bayou is good for that.

The 42 campsites are situated on a large, paved loop road that passes through a sand pine forest. Both sand pine and longleaf pine mix in with live oaks to make a shady campground. A thick understory of yaupon holly, wax myrtle, and saw palmetto combine to provide fine campsite privacy. A few southern magnolias add to the flora.

The camping area is mostly flat, with a very slight slope angling toward Rocky Bayou. The first 11 campsites on the outside of the loop are nonelectric. These sites are also the largest. This is where tent campers will want to be. The 14 sites across the road are more compact and have electricity. These are the less-desirable sites in which to stay.

As the loop turns, you'll pass the short pathway to the nature trails and Puddin' Head Lake. The next 11 campsites are on the inside of the loop. They are electric and close together. This is where the RVs like to congregate. These campsites have the advantage of overlooking Rocky Bayou across a grassy lawn. There is also a picnic

CAMPGROUND RATINGS

Beauty: ★★★★
Site privacy: ★★★
Site spaciousness: ★★★★
Quiet: ★★
Security: ★★★★
Cleanliness/upkeep: ★★★★

The spacious, nonelectric campsites and winding nature trails complement this relaxed, saltwater getaway.

pavilion for campers near a swimming beach.

The road passes the older, but clean, comfort station on the inside of the loop, then comes to six more campsites on the inside of the loop. If you plan to tent camp but want electricity, stay here.

Rocky Bayou Campground is quiet most of the year. During the winter, travelers will use it as a stopover spot. The campground starts to get busy in mid-March and stays full on warm weekends until September. Weekdays during

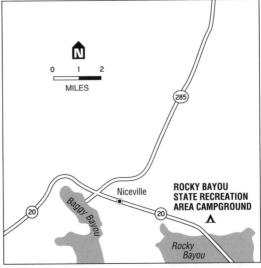

this time are about half full. So unless you arrive at the campground at 5 P.M. on a warm Saturday, you are likely to find a good campsite.

Rocky Bayou has over a mile of shoreline to enjoy. There are two primary swimming areas: down from the campground pavilion at the campground and near the picnic area. You'll need to watch the littler swimmers as there is no lifeguard on duty. Anglers have their own launch to access the saltwater species swimming about Rocky Bayou.

I personally liked Puddin' Head Lake. With a name like that, what's there not to love? It was created by beavers—you can see the dam just steps away from the campground. The water is clear and full of freshwater fish. If you bring a canoe, you'll probably bring out fish.

Another way to check out Puddin' Head Lake is the Sand Pine Trail. Make sure and stop by the Ranger Station to get the well-written handout for the Rocky Bayou nature trails. Sand Pine Trail skirts the eastern edge of the lake. Look for fish in the water, and don't miss the second beaver dam on the upper stretches of the lake.

The Rocky Bayou Trail starts at Puddin' Head Lake and makes its own loop. Part of the trail winds along the waters of Rocky Bayou. The Red Cedar Trail begins near the picnic area and traverses an area of southern magnolia, sand pine, live oak, and, of course, red cedar.

If you want to get right on the beach, take the midbay bridge, State Road 293, over to Henderson Beach State Recreation Area in Destin. It has the famed sugar-white sand beaches for which this area is known. Picnic shelters and bathhouses are provided for your comfort.

Rocky Bayou Campground has the advantages of saltwater without all the saltwater crowds. You can enjoy the Gulf and return here. And at Rocky Bayou, there is ample recreation without ever leaving your campsite.

To get there from Niceville, take SR 20 east for 5 miles. Rocky Bayou State Recreation Area will be on your left.

KEY INFORMATION

Rocky Bayou Campground
4281 Highway 20
Niceville, FL 32578

Operated by: Florida State Parks

Information: (904) 833-9144

Open: Year-round

Individual sites: 31 electric, 11 nonelectric

Each site has: Picnic table, fire ring, water

Site assignment: First come, first served; no reservations

Registration: At Ranger Station between 4 and 5 P.M.

Facilities: Hot showers, flush toilets, pay phone

Parking: At campsites only

Fee: $8 per night; $2 electricity fee

Elevation: Sea level

Restrictions

Pets—Prohibited

Fires—In fire rings only

Alcoholic beverages—Prohibited

Vehicles—None

Other—14-day stay limit

41

ST. ANDREWS CAMPGROUND

Panama City

St. Andrews Recreation Area has superior natural features but a large, average campground. The blue-and-green waters contrast brilliantly with the white beach. Shell Island, one of the few pristine barrier islands left, is one of the best examples of the real, natural Florida in the state. The campground has its share of good sites, but it is so big it sometimes seems like a city of its own.

There are two campgrounds that are really so close that they are more like one. In general, the camping area is beneath a pine forest between Grand Lagoon and some old sand dunes. Saw palmetto forms a light understory. The campground is open and you can see from one site to the next. A recent road repaving caused many trees to be cut down, but there is adequate shade overhead.

The first area is called Lagoon Campground. It has 100 campsites. Thirty-one sites are waterfront. Some are directly on the water and others have a section of saw grass between the water and the campsite. The campsites away from the water abut some attractive sand dunes that provide shade but cut down on the ocean breeze, which can be good or bad, according to the season.

There is one loop in the Grand Lagoon. The 22 campsites on the inside of the loop are well forested, but they have neither a dune by them nor a waterfront view. Two fully equipped comfort stations serve the

CAMPGROUND RATINGS

Beauty: ★★★★
Site privacy: ★★★
Site spaciousness: ★★★
Quiet: ★★
Security: ★★★★★
Cleanliness/upkeep: ★★★★

Sugar-white beaches and a pristine barrier island can be found at St. Andrews State Recreation Area.

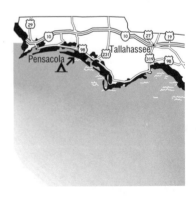

lagoon campground. Overall, the campsites in the Lagoon Campground are smaller and closer together than the sites in the Pine Grove Campground.

Pine Grove Campground has 75 campsites. Twenty-two campsites are waterfront. This area has recently been burned over; the undergrowth is coming back and eventually will be thicker. There are three separate loops in Pine Grove. Each loop has its own fully equipped comfort station; the farthest loop has laundry facilities as well.

The 30 campsites on the inside of the loops have the least privacy. The farthest loop has an odd configuration of campsites that allow the most privacy, especially in such a large campground that is going to have a significant amount of casual drive-by traffic.

St. Andrews is busy from March, when the college spring-breakers come, through the summer, when vacationing families take over. Starting in September, the campground slows back down. Winter has its share of "snowbirds." This is when the number of RVs will be at its peak. Unfortunately, tents and RVs aren't separated.

When you come to St. Andrews, ask to drive through the campground to select your site. There are campsites that range from superb to some real dogs. That is the only problem when you reserve a site by phone—you can't pick your site. However, once you arrive, you can try to change to a better campsite. Be aware of the fact that the campground is not some all-natural experience. It looks out over the civilized mainland.

Once here, you'll see why so many other campers have joined you. Take the mandatory walk on the beach. Huge dunes rise around the jetty area. From atop the dunes you can see the water colors that range from green to blue as the water depth changes. These dunes descend to water level.

Across the jetty is Shell Island. In the warmer months, a ferry runs to the island every 30 minutes. This place is the get-away from the getaway. It is 7 miles around the island. The farther you get from St. Andrews, the more isolated Shell Island gets. This is what Florida used to look like before time-share condos and T-shirt shops took over. Simply put, it's spectacular.

The main beach is where swimmers and sunbathers congregate. Behind the jetty is a swimming area without all the wave action. Fishermen can be seen on the jetty, the Gulf fishing pier, and the Grand Lagoon fishing pier.

If you get tired of walking the beach, try the Gator Lake Nature Trail or the Pine Flatwoods Nature Trail. Both are short walks through oceanside ecosystems. Be sure to check out the old turpentine still. It is located near the boat ramp that extends into Grand Lagoon. Canoes are also for rent here. If you forgot supplies, there is a park store that sells goodies and ice.

Though the campground at St. Andrews is big, the natural beauty is big, too. Just pick a good campsite and remember that the campground isn't as big as most of the places where we live.

To get there from Panama City, drive west on U.S. 98, cross the bridge over West Bay, and continue a short distance to CR 3031. Turn left on CR 3031 and follow it 4 miles to CR 392. Turn left on CR 392 and shortly dead-end into St. Andrews State Recreation Area.

KEY INFORMATION

St. Andrews Campground
4607 State Park Lane
Panama City, FL 32408

Operated by: Florida State Parks

Information: (904) 233-5140

Open: Year-round

Individual sites: 176

Each site has: Picnic table, fire ring, water, electricity

Site assignment: Assigned by ranger

Registration: By phone or at park entrance booth

Facilities: Hot showers, flush toilets, pay phone, camp store, laundry

Parking: At campsites only

Fee: $8 per night October to February, $15 per night March to September; $2 waterfront site; $2 electricity fee

Elevation: Sea level

Restrictions

Pets—Prohibited

Fires—In fire rings only

Alcoholic beverages—Prohibited

Vehicles—None

Other—14-day stay limit

FLORIDA PANHANDLE

ST. GEORGE ISLAND CAMPGROUND

Apalachicola

The eastern end of St. George Island is sand, sea, and sky. As you drive into the entrance, white sand blows across the road and waves roll up on the beach. Patches of sea oats cling to the dunes. Sunlight reflects off land and water. Beach lovers can really appreciate this park. If only the campground matched the scenery of St. George Island.

That is not to say the campground isn't worth pitching a tent. It is. It just doesn't match the raw beauty of St. George Island State Park. Turn left onto the campground road 4 miles beyond the park entrance. You'll pass a marsh and enter the long, narrow campground loop. It has 60 campsites; all but 11 are on the outside of the loop.

The campground has an open feel, even though there are tall slash pines scattered about. The first 28 sites back up to a pine flatwoods that changes to marshy wetland. The holly known as yaupon grows in clumps to break up the campground. Tall grass grows right up to some campsites that abut the marsh. These sites have a buggy look to them.

As the loop curves around, the campsites are nearer to the dunes. Small pine trees and hodgepodge clumps of brush divide the sites, yet the area still conveys a feel of openness. Campsite privacy is compromised somewhat. Adequate space is provided for all campsites at St. George. The campsites in the center of the loop are even

CAMPGROUND RATINGS

Beauty: ★★★
Site privacy: ★★★
Site spaciousness: ★★★
Quiet: ★★★★
Security: ★★★★★
Cleanliness/upkeep: ★★★★

Miles of beaches await tent campers who come to this barrier island.

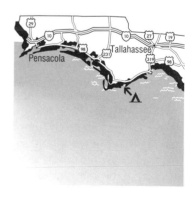

45

more open. They are next to the two fully equipped camper bathhouses. Crushed oyster shells and grass form the ground cover for the campground.

Some rangers at St. George are trying to hold campsites 50 through 60 for tent campers only. This puts like-minded campers together; this way you won't be stuck between two rolling houses. But this policy is not an official policy. You probably won't see too many RVs except during the winter months when "snow-

birds" use St. George Island as a stopover spot while heading for points farther south.

Remember to store your food properly here. Bold raccoons will come out during the day and rob you of your precious goodies. During my visit, I saw three racoons raiding a campsite while the tenants were away.

After you've stored your food away, the first place you should head for is the beach. It is very wide and 9 miles long. Beachcombers can walk until their legs fail them. Dunes rise and fall on the narrow spit of land. If you really want to get wild, walk to East Point. It is the most pristine part of the island and very inaccessible since Hurricane Opal wiped out the last 3 miles of road. Plans call for a four-wheel-drive road to go closer to East Point. But for now, it's just you, the sand, and the sea. Fishing is very good out at the point. The views over Apalachicola Sound, the Gulf and nearby Dog Island are worth the walk. Anglers can catch flounder, redfish, whiting, and sea trout.

Shade-seeking woodland hikers can take the 2.5-mile trail out to Gap Point. This trail passes through a live oak hammock and pine flatwoods. It starts at the back of the campground loop. Remember, this is a one-way hike.

You may see some birds here. There are native feathered friends, such as terns and plovers, and many migratory visitors making St. George a stopover spot. The campground sounded like a winged singalong when I was there.

If you leave the island, go to Apalachicola for some fresh seafood. All the water around you, Apalachicola Bay, is some of the world's most productive waters for oysters and other edible sea critters. You can't get seafood much fresher than you will get it in Apalachicola. Plus, you will get to take in some of the native culture. It's a Southern country town by the sea. While you are in town, visit the John Gorrie Museum. He invented the ice machine. It's all part of the St. George Island experience.

To **get there** from Apalachicola, drive east on U.S. 98 and cross John Gorrie Memorial Bridge. Turn right on CR 300 and cross St. George Sound to St. George Island. Then turn left on Gulf Beach Drive and follow it for 4 miles to the dead end at St. George Island State Park.

KEY INFORMATION

St. George Island Campground
HCR Box 62
St. George Island, FL 32328

Operated by: Florida State Parks

Information: (904) 927-2111

Open: Year-round

Individual sites: 60

Each site has: Picnic table, fire ring, water, electricity

Site assignment: Assigned by ranger unless specific site asked for

Registration: By phone or at park entrance booth

Facilities: Hot showers, flush toilets, pay phone

Parking: At campsites and extra car parking

Fee: $9 per night September through January, $15 per night February through August; $2 electricity fee

Elevation: Sea level

Restrictions

Pets—Prohibited

Fires—In fire rings only

Alcoholic beverages—Prohibited

Vehicles—None

Other—14-day stay limit

ST. JOSEPH PENINSULA CAMPGROUND

Port St. Joe

St. Joseph Peninsula State Park is a narrow spit of land that juts out into the Gulf of Mexico. It is surrounded on three sides by water. A wilderness preserve covers the last 1,650 acres of the sliver of land. The huge sand dunes and miles of beach and woods will beckon your call. One of the two park campgrounds is ideal for tent campers.

As you drive on the narrow expanse of land, you can see water on both sides. You wonder, where are they going to put a campground? Soon you come to Camping Area I. It has 59 campsites in an open area between a marsh and sand dunes. Pine trees grow about the area, but it is not a forest by any means. The center of the loop is grassy with a smattering of palms. The outer part of the loop is sandy, with a light understory. The campsites are wide enough to pull an RV in. Two crossroads bisect the loop so RVs can pull in and out.

There is a single bathhouse for this loop. The only advantage this area has over the other camping area is its proximity to the beach, but the difference is negligible compared with the negatives of this loop. Stay here only if there are no other sites in the other loop.

Camp Area II is farther into the park. The campsite ratings are for this loop only. It has 51 campsites in a thick forest of longleaf pine, coastal live oak, and sabal palm, stretched out on an oval loop. Attractive,

CAMPGROUND RATINGS

Beauty:	★★★★★
Site privacy:	★★★★
Site spaciousness:	★★
Quiet:	★★★
Security:	★★★★★
Cleanliness/upkeep:	★★★★

St. Joseph has great oceanside camping and a wilderness preserve, too.

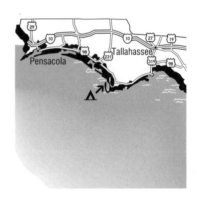

sizable campsites are on either side of the loop. A dense understory of palmetto, yaupon, and other brush rises high and shields the campsites from one another. Wherever there's no brush, there is grass.

Once you get halfway along the loop, the nonelectric sites begin. This often divides tent and RV campers, but not at this loop. The forest and brush is simply too thick here to drive an RV into. So you can tent camp and use electricity here without fear of being scrunched between two moving houses.

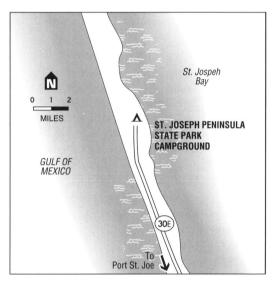

Nearly all of the campsites on the second half of Camp Area II are on the inside of the loop. They can be quite hemmed in by the brush, yet that is a positive trait. Four larger campsites are on the outside of the loop in a low spot that could prove uncomfortable during a rainstorm. The only negative of these sites is a subdued ocean breeze. Two comfort stations serve this entire loop. Warning: Do not leave any food out here; the raccoons are persistent and sneaky.

It is just a short walk from either campground to the beach. Here you will find miles of white sand, bordered by some of the highest dunes in Florida. Walk until you find you own relaxation spot. Surf-fishing can be done in the Gulf or St. Joseph Bay. Sea trout fishing in the bay can be excellent. If you like to hunt for shells, go to the bay side. I have never seen so many sand dollars in one place in all of my life.

There is a boat launch at the marina, where canoes can be rented as well. A ranger has to approve the rental of a canoe, which is dependent on water conditions. Two nature trails serve the park. The Bay Trail leaves the picnic area and explores the woods and marsh of the bay side of the peninsula. The Coastal Hammock Trail starts at the park entrance and winds through an ocean-side woodland that is rapidly disappearing in areas surrounding it.

But the primary exploratory attraction is the St. Joseph Wilderness Preserve. It covers the northern 5 miles of the peninsula and has the biggest sand dunes of them all. A freshwater marsh waters wildlife such as deer, raccoon, gray fox, and bobcat. Birders will be rewarded with sightings, too.

There are three ways to explore the preserve. You can walk the Gulf beach, the more difficult bay beach, or the center of the island via an old fire road. I've done the all and like to hike the fire road best. This is because other roads split off it and you can reach the Gulf or the bay depending on your whim. You can even devise a loop of you own. The fire road starts at the end of the cabin road.

Every season offers something special here. Get reservations on spring and summer weekends. Fall can be a special time with warm days and cool nights. Winter offers solitude. No matter when you come here, you should have a wonderful experience.

To get there from Port St. Joe, go east on U.S. 98. Go 3 miles. Turn right on CR 30 and follow it for 8 miles. Take the sharp right turn on CR 30E and follow it for 9 miles. You will dead-end into the road.

KEY INFORMATION

St. Joseph Peninsula Campground
8899 Cape San Blas Road
Port St. Joe, FL 32456

Operated by: Florida State Parks

Information: (904) 227-1327

Open: Year-round

Individual sites: 97 electric, 23 nonelectric

Each site has: Picnic table, fire ring, water spigot

Site assignment: Assigned by ranger unless specific site asked for

Registration: By phone or at park entrance booth

Facilities: Hot showers, flush toilets, pay phone

Parking: At campsite only

Fee: $8 per night November to February, $15 per night March to October; $2 electricity fee

Elevation: Sea level

Restrictions

   Pets—Prohibited

   Fires—In fire rings only

   Alcoholic beverages—Prohibited

   Vehicles—None

SILVER LAKE CAMPGROUND

Tallahassee

Silver Lake is a popular, summer day use area and has an old but attractive campground that is being improved by the Forest Service. The 23-acre spring-fed lake is ringed by forest. The campground was once much larger. It has been reduced and makes for a good place to stay any time of the year.

As you pass the road to the campground host's site, you'll begin the teardrop-shaped loop road of Silver Lake Campground. Campsites begin on both sides of the road. Overhead, a forest of laurel oak and pine have matured and make for a shady campground. The sites are large and set back from the road.

Oak seedlings and other brush form good campsite buffers. Most campsites are on the outside of the loop and have more privacy. As the road loops around, the old, abandoned campground loop can be seen on the right. It is being reclaimed by the forest.

The center of the campground has a block-style bathroom with flush toilets for each sex. It is almost obscured by woodland. The cold showers are in a walled enclosure with no roof. The walls provide privacy, but you are at the mercy of the elements above when you clean up here. The bathroom does have a roof, however.

The campsites have even more privacy as the 30-site loop comes to a close. Some of the campsites have old concrete picnic tables; others have new ones. This camp-

CAMPGROUND RATINGS

Beauty:	★★★
Site privacy:	★★★
Site spaciousness:	★★★★
Quiet:	★★★
Security:	★★★
Cleanliness/upkeep:	★★★

There is much to see in the Silver Lake area of the Apalachicola National Forest.

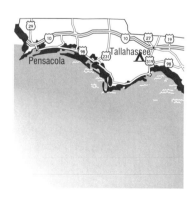

ground is being revamped in a piecemeal process. Expect it to continue to improve.

The whole recreation area is centered around Silver Lake. The lake has picnic facilities and a swimming beach. The fishing is said to be productive. It will be a peaceful and relaxing endeavor no matter what—gas-powered motors are not allowed on Silver Lake. Canoeists can paddle for pleasure, or maybe obtain dinner with rod and reel.

Moore Lake and Bradford Brook are just down Forest

Road 370 from Silver Lake. Bradford Brook makes an ideal paddle on a cypress-ringed lake and creek. It has very little current, making a there-and-back paddle possible for all canoeists.

Hikers can take the Silver Lake Nature Trail. It starts near the swimming beach by the lake. One of the most unusual features in the Apalachicola National Forest, Leon Sinks, is nearby. It is an area of many sinkholes where the limestone below has crumbled and the land fallen in. The plant life can be very unusual in these sinks. Other sinks are watery. The Leon Sinks parking area is off U.S. 319.

There are two major trails at Leon Sinks: the Sinkhole Trail and the Gumswamp Trail. The 3.1-mile Sinkhole Trail passes around and through no less than 17 sinks. Some are wet, some dry. Fisher Creek disappears then reappears farther downstream. Cross the creek on the Natural Bridge. The 2.3-mile Gumswamp Trail passes a wet sink known as the Gopher Hole and meanders through a swamp area to meet the Crossover Trail at Fisher Creek Sink.

Hunting is prohibited in this area, enhancing your chances of seeing wildlife. As you walk, remember that below you is a world of water-filled caves that are part of this whole geological area known as the Woodville Karst Plain.

Also close to Silver Lake is Trout Pond. This is a small scenic body of water near Leon Sinks on County Road 373. It has a fishing pier and is a model for universally accessible recreation areas. The Discovery National Recreation Trail starts in the picnic area.

Silver Lake is an old campground being rebuilt. It is already good and will get even better. The camping is in an attractive forest and makes a good base camp for exploring the northeastern corner of the Apalachicola National Forest. The university town and state capital of Tallahassee is just minutes away for supply runs and for urban recreating.

To get there from Tallahassee, drive to the intersection of Hwys. 263 and 20. Follow Hwy. 20 west for 4 miles. Turn left on CR 260 and follow it for 4 miles. Turn left at the Silver Lake sign. The campground will be on your left once you enter the gates.

KEY INFORMATION

Silver Lake Campground
State Highway 20
P.O. Box 579
Bristol, FL 32321

Operated by: U.S. Forest Service

Information: (904) 926-3561

Open: Year-round

Individual sites: 30

Each site has: Picnic table, fire ring

Site assignment: First come, first served; no reservations

Registration: Self-registration on site

Facilities: Cold showers, flush toilets, water spigots

Parking: At campsites only

Fee: $8 per night

Elevation: 80 feet

Restrictions

Pets—On 6-foot leash only

Fires—In fire rings only

Alcoholic beverages—Prohibited

Vehicles—None

Other—14-day stay limit

TORREYA CAMPGROUND

Bristol

Natural vistas are uncommon in Florida. Torreya is loaded with them; even the campground sports a great view. These high bluffs are located along the Apalachicola River. Their inclines support hardwoods more commonly seen in the Southern Appalachian Mountains. The park is also the home of the rare Torreya tree that grows only this area. If that isn't enough, this surprising state park is home of the antebellum Gregory House, where tours will open your eyes to Panhandle plantation life.

The Weeping Ridge Camping Area is a peaceful island surrounded on three sides by steep bluffs. Thirty-one campsites spur off the outside of the teardrop-shaped, sand loop road. The tall forest overhead is a mixture of pine, live oak, and a few other hardwoods. Weeping Ridge is fairly open on the ground level. But landscaped campsite buffers have been planted to increase campsite privacy. These trees and bushes add to an already attractive setting.

The first 16 campsites have electrical hookups. They are fairly close to one another but extend far back from the road, creating long and narrow campsites. Each site backs up to a bluff.

Just beyond the 16th campsite, the sand road curves and opens up to a rare Florida vista. A grassy yard with two benches lies beneath some really large hardwoods. To your north is an expanse

CAMPGROUND RATINGS

Beauty:	★★★★
Site privacy:	★★★
Site spaciousness:	★★★
Quiet:	★★★★★
Security:	★★★★★
Cleanliness/upkeep:	★★★★

High bluffs and rare vegetation complement this attractive campground with a view.

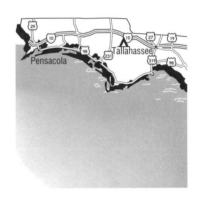

of land and distance that beck-ons you to scan the horizon.

Past the vista is the begin-ning of the nonelectric sites. These are much wider, yet every bit as deep as the electric sites. These sites back up to a bluff as well. A comfort station interrupts the sequence of campsites on the outside of the loop. The comfort station is a little on the old side, but it's clean and functional.

The final six campsites are the largest in the campground. They have sizable grassy areas beneath the trees. If you have a

large family or a lot of gear, then these sites are for you. There is also a special treat for those who camp here—one of the rare Torreya trees lies along the road between campsites 28 and 29. The small evergreen can be identified by its unusual needles.

The center of the campground has a grassy lawn beneath the pines. It hous-es the meetinghouse, which hosts infrequent camp functions and doubles as the registration location. Torreya State Park is rarely busy. It lies at the end of a road in a rural area. This makes for a quiet, peaceful camping experience.

The first thing to do once you set up camp is to visit the Gregory House. This house was actually across the Apalachicola River at one time. It was moved to its present location in the 1930s. The plantation of Jason Gregory was built in 1849 and thrived on slave labor until the Civil War. It is furnished with items from the 1850s; it's worth your time to take the ranger-led tour. The tour is offered at 10 A.M. weekdays and three times on weekends. The view from the back of the house looks down on the river and the former location of the house.

From the back of the house you can take the Apalachicola River Bluffs Trail, designated a National Recreation Trail. It drops down off the steep bluff and passes old Confederate gun pits that once protected the river route, important in those times. The trail leads right down along the river itself.

The park has two long-distance trails, thanks to a recent land acquisition. There are two loops, approximately 7 miles each. They both pass through the many plant communities represented in the park and have more hills than just about any other hiking trail in the state.

A shorter trail starts right at the campground. The Weeping Ridge Trail leads down a bluff to a small waterfall. I walked this little gem early in the morning, after a significant rain. The little falls was dropping for all it was worth.

I came back to the nearly abandoned campground wondering why more people didn't come here. The hilly terrain is unusual for the state. The rare Torreya tree, along with another rare evergreen, the Florida yew, make this place special. As a matter of fact, the world-record Florida yew is in this park. If you like a little human history and a lot of nature, complete with a quiet, attractive campground, come to Torreya State Park.

To get there from Bristol, take FL 12 north for 6 miles. Turn left on CR 271 and follow it for 3 miles to CR 270. Turn left onto CR 270 and follow it for 3 miles to Torreya State Park.

KEY INFORMATION

Torreya Campground
HC 2, Box 70
Bristol, FL 32321

Operated by: Florida State Parks

Information: (904) 643-2674

Open: Year-round

Individual sites: 16 electric, 15 nonelectric

Each site has: Picnic table, fire ring, water

Site assignment: First come, first served; no reservations

Registration: At campground meetinghouse

Facilities: Hot showers, flush toilets, electrical hookups

Parking: At campsites only

Fee: $8 per night; $2 electricity fee

Elevation: 250 feet

Restrictions

 Pets—Prohibited

 Fires—In fire rings only

 Alcoholic beverages—Prohibited

 Vehicles—None

 Other—14-day stay limit

FLORIDA PANHANDLE

WRIGHT LAKE CAMPGROUND

Sumatra

Wright Lake Campground has been completely revamped by the Forest Service. Far from the civilized world, Wright Lake is a well-kept secret among locals and those who stumble onto it. This campground offers the best of two worlds. It is in a remote section of a scenic national forest but has the amenities of a more developed campground. There are outdoor activities within walking and driving distance.

Once you find Wright Lake Campground, you will see why national forest aficionados come back time and again. It is on a side road off a dead-end road. The campground is in a teardrop-shaped loop beneath a stately forest of mature pines. A parklike openness below the pines is broken up by patches of underbrush and small laurel oaks. Grass and pine needles carpet the camping area.

There are only 20 campsites, but there is enough room for 40. Space is no problem here. The daunting size alone of the campground means more site privacy. The seven campsites on the inside of the loop are more open. Thick brush separates most of the campsites on the outside of the loop. There has even been some tastefully decorative landscaping of Wright Lake since its makeover.

Everything at each campsite has been replaced—fire ring, grill, picnic table, water spigot, and lantern post. All the sites

CAMPGROUND RATINGS

Beauty:	★★★★
Site privacy:	★★★
Site spaciousness:	★★★★★
Quiet:	★★★★★
Security:	★★★
Cleanliness/upkeep:	★★★★

Wright Lake is the prettiest campground in the Apalachicola National Forest.

---

are appealing, but water lovers may want to get the last four sites on the outside of the loop. They back up to Wright Lake.

A new comfort station centers the loop. It has warm-water showers, flush toilets, and is a state-of-the-art, national forest comfort station. Most of the old-timers at the campground liked the changes. They had seen it evolve from a free but rough camping area to the Appalachicola National Forest's best campground.

I have seen it change myself and have been pleasantly surprised. I am of the opinion that you can't improve on the works of nature. Yet, Wright Lake Campground proves to me that you can tastefully integrate the works of man into the works of nature.

With such a fine campground, the Forest Service had to come up with recreation to match. They have constructed the Wright Lake Trail, a 4.5-mile loop that covers the most interesting terrain in the area. The trail starts in the picnic area by the lake. The board at the beginning of the trail thoroughly explains each ecosystem, from cypress swamp to pine woods. It also shows where to look for wildlife as you walk this trail. The trail makes a beeline for Owl Creek, then skirts several ponds, crosses pine flatwoods, and reemerges at Wright Lake. The Wright Lake Loop Trails travel a quarter mile and intersects the campground. Watch for red-cockaded woodpeckers, but you'll probably hear them before you see them.

Wright Lake is small but scenic. It doesn't even have a boat launch. This natural lake is made for canoes. Since there is very little direct land access for the lake, paddlers have the advantage when it comes to casting their line for bream, bass, and catfish.

Nearby Owl Creek is swamp canoeing at its best. Put in at Hickory Landing, just down the road, and paddle upstream or downstream. Kennedy Creek, accessible from Cotton Landing, is also a great place for remote canoeing. Both creeks flow into the Apalachicola River and have angling opportunities of their own.

Make sure to bring all of the supplies you will need. The hamlet of Sumatra has one small store and it is a good one-hour drive to a town of any size. If you must drive, take the Apalachee Savannahs Scenic Byway. It is State Road 12 through the national forest. The open, wet meadows are botanically rich. South of Wright Lake on the Byway is Fort Gadsden Historic Site. Here you'll find a museum that tells of the strategic importance of the Apalachicola River.

Wright Lake is a place to come to again and again. Just try to keep it a secret—once you find it.

To get there from Sumatra, take State Highway 65 south for 2 miles. Turn right on FS 101 and drive for about 2 miles. Turn right on FS 101-C and follow it for about 0.3 mile. Wright Lake will be on your right.

KEY INFORMATION

Wright Lake Campground
State Highway 20
P.O. Box 579
Bristol, FL 32321

Operated by: U.S. Forest Service

Information: (904) 643-2282

Open: Year-round

Individual sites: 20

Each site has: Tent pad, picnic table, fire ring, grill, water spigot, lantern post

Site assignment: First come, first served; no reservations

Registration: Self-registration on-site

Facilities: Warm showers, flush toilets

Parking: At campsites only

Fee: $6 per night

Elevation: 20 feet

Restrictions

Pets—On 6-foot leash only

Fires—In fire rings only

Alcoholic beverages—Prohibited

Vehicles—None

Other—14-day stay limit

NORTH
FLORIDA

ANASTASIA CAMPGROUND

St. Augustine

St. Augustine is noted for being the oldest city in America. Anastasia State Recreation Area should be noted for its campground set in a coastal hammock, its unspoiled beaches, and general marine character.

The 139 campsites suggest a large campground, but Anastasia is divided into seven distinct loops, all enveloped in the thickness of the coastal woods. These woods make each loop feels like its own distinct campground. The unusual forest is a product of its proximity to the ocean. Live oak is the primary tree here, but it's crowded by the smaller laurel oak. Palms fight for space and light, along with red cedar and southern magnolia. The bushy understory is primarily a plant called yaupon; it is a type of holly that makes an ideal campsite buffer. All this flora makes for a distinctly Florida forest.

As you pass the tiny camp store, you'll see the first loop, Coquina, on your left. Don't even bother—it's RV headquarters. Turn right to access the other six loops. All of the loops on the main campground road run east-west in a long and narrow pattern. Two loops each share a comfort station, located between them. The comfort stations all have hot showers and flush toilets.

After Coquina, the next two loops are Sea Bean and Queen Conch. They are the only nonelectric loops in Anastasia. Like many other Florida state parks, these are the undesignated tent campers' loops. The sites offer

CAMPGROUND RATINGS

Beauty:	★★★★
Site privacy:	★★★★
Site spaciousness:	★★★
Quiet:	★★★
Security:	★★★★★
Cleanliness/upkeep:	★★★★

Near the oldest city in America, Anastasia offers camping in a maritime forest within walking distance to the beach.

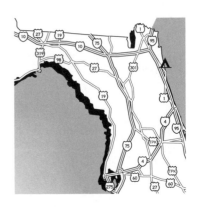

the best in campsite privacy because of the denseness of the maritime forest. However, the thick forest cuts down on site spaciousness, but the trade-off is more than worth it.

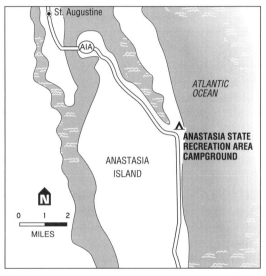

The next two loops, Shark Eye and Sand Dollar, have larger campsites and offer a mixed bag of tents, pop-ups, and a few RVs. The final two loops, Sea Urchin and Angel Wing, are much the same. These loops all share that beautiful, coastal hammock forest. For some reason, many campers like the few sites at the narrow curve of each loop the best. They are closest to the ocean but don't have an ocean view or direct ocean access. Maybe these campers can hear the waves better.

Early spring to late September is the more popular time here, as reflected by the increase in campsite price. Not many "snowbirds" set up camp here because it is too far north. Winter days can be very mild or cool. It's worth taking a chance, though, for solitude seekers. Summer weekend campers are advised to get a campsite reservation in advance for peace of mind. Once securing a campsite, you can concentrate on what you are going to do when you get here.

The beach is the main focus at Anastasia. Although it is a short walk from the campground to the Atlantic, you can actually drive on the beach to your chosen spot if you want to. The beach is wide here and is backed by partially vegetated sand dunes. Swimmers, sunbathers, and beachcombers all find Anastasia to their liking. The northern end of the beach is for fishermen, who surf-cast for pompano and whiting.

The tidal lagoon behind the beach is popular, too. No swimming is allowed here in Salt Run, but canoes and wind-surfing rigs are for rent. People fish for flounder, redfish, and sea trout in the calmer waters.

After you have received your fill of the beach, check in on the history here. A lesser-known but very interesting site is the Fort Matanzas National Monument. I enjoyed this side trip immensely. It is south of Anastasia on A1A. Matanzas is an old fort built in the 1700s by the British. A free boat tour takes you to the fort; a narrator gives an overview of this tower that once protected St. Augustine's back door.

Now you have to go to St. Augustine itself. There is another fort to see right in town, and trams will take you to see the primary sights. Then get out and walk around on your own. St. Augustine may be the oldest city in America, but it is certainly not the biggest. The city retains its small-town charm.

The windswept coastal forest, the lure of the beach, and the sense of history all combine to make Anastasia a worthwhile stop for anyone coming to the Sunshine State.

To **get there** from St. Augustine, drive south on A1A over the Bridge of Lions for 4 miles. Anastasia State Recreation Area will be on your left.

KEY INFORMATION

**Anastasia Campground
1340 A1A South
St. Augustine, FL 32084**

Operated by: Florida State Parks

Information: (904) 461-2033

Open: Year-round

Individual sites: 139

Each site has: Picnic table, fire ring, water spigot

Site assignment: Assigned by ranger unless specific site asked for

Registration: By phone or at park entrance booth

Facilities: Hot showers, flush toilets, pay phone, camp store

Parking: At campsites and extra car parking

Fee: $16.50 per night March to September, $13 per night October to February; $2 electricity fee

Elevation: Sea level

Restrictions

   Pets—Prohibited

   Fires—In fire rings only

   Alcoholic beverages—Prohibited

   Vehicles—None

FAVER-DYKES CAMPGROUND

St. Augustine

It had been a long day of driving when I came to the turn to Faver-Dykes State Park. One of the two enormous fruit stand/gas stations at the turn lured me in. I stopped here for the second-to-last time that day to load up on fresh Indian River citrus. The road turned sandy upon entering the park and began to tunnel through a luxuriant forest. I hoped the campground would be as pretty.

It was. A thick forest of live oak, pignut hickory, and southern magnolia kept the campground well shaded. Spanish moss, palm trees, and palmetto gave the campground the tropical look that Florida natives and outlanders alike associate with Sunshine State woodlands. Thick undergrowth made nearly every campsite private and appealing. It was going to be hard to decide which campsite to pick. A hot shower in the comfort station was calling me to rid the road grime from my body.

While driving around the campground loop, it became apparent that there were no unoccupied campsites. I was too exhausted to drive on and the campground was appealing. At the end of the loop was the campground host. When I told him of my dilemma, he contacted a ranger on his walkie-talkie and they located an overflow spot for me. What a relief! This was an example of how helpful campground hosts can be and how courteous the Florida State Park rangers are.

CAMPGROUND RATINGS

Beauty: ★★★★
Site privacy: ★★★
Site spaciousness: ★★★
Quiet: ★★★★
Security: ★★★★
Cleanliness/upkeep: ★★★★

The campground at Faver-Dykes makes a good stopover camp from I-95 or a tranquil locale to snooze beneath a lush woodland.

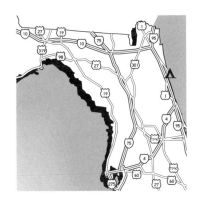

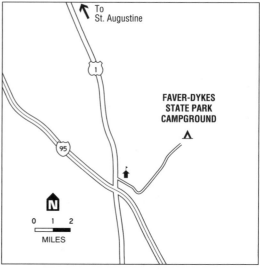

Throughout my research for this guidebook, I explored every state park in Florida that had a campground (and a few that didn't). I found park employees to be a major asset to this state's park system. They had the patience to answer my endless questions and worked hard enough to dispel my image of lazy government employees. But I'll have to say, employees in the Keys parks can become a bit aggravated at times.

Anyway, I pitched my tent and drove back to the picnic area on Pellicer Creek. A sandy-floored forest of pines shaded the picnic area. Boardwalks led out to the marsh and water of Pellicer Creek. I peeled and ate an Indian River tangerine as the sun descended to a fiery ball over the marsh, an exellent birding spot. I was scouting it for canoeing and fishing possibilities.

A section of Pellicer Creek is designated as a Florida Canoe Trail. The 4-mile paddle starts at Faver-Dykes and heads toward the coast. It is a user-friendly stream because you can paddle there and back. Try to time your trip with the tides. The brackish water holds sea trout, redfish, sheepshead, and flounder. You can rent a canoe here, but you'll need a reservation because rangers are hard to find. There is no on-site Ranger Station at Faver-Dykes.

A small fishing pier extends onto the creek for nonboaters. Two short nature trails will enhance your appreciation of the park. The attractive picnic area is worth toting a meal over from the campground.

For me, Faver-Dykes was a stopover location. But most of the campers told me they came here for relaxation. The favored times to visit are all but the coolest spells of winter. Early spring and late fall can be gorgeous. Summer can be really hot and buggy. But Faver-Dykes makes a really cheap bedding spot for tourists who want to visit nearby St. Augustine, Marineland, or Daytona Beach.

Other attractions within reasonable driving distance are Washington Oaks State Gardens and Fort Matanzas National Monument. I highly recommend the boat ride to tour the old, lonely fort by St. Augustine's back door. The beach at Washington Oaks is preserved in its natural state. The nearest beach town is Crescent Beach, north of Faver-Dykes off U.S. 1.

To get there from St. Augustine, drive south on U.S. 1 for 17 miles to I-95. Just before you reach I-95, turn left at the sign for Faver-Dykes State Park. The road will dead-end into the state park.

KEY INFORMATION

Faver-Dykes Campground
1000 Faver-Dykes Road
St. Augustine, FL 32086

Operated by: Florida State Parks

Information: (904) 794-0997

Open: Year-round

Individual sites: 30

Each site has: Picnic table, fire ring, water, electricity

Site assignment: First come, first served; no reservations

Registration: Self-registration on site

Facilities: Hot showers, flush toilets

Parking: At campsites only

Fee: $8 per night; $2 electricity fee

Elevation: 5 feet

Restrictions

Pets—Prohibited

Fires—In fire rings only

Alcoholic beverages—Prohibited

Vehicles—None

FORT CLINCH CAMPGROUND

Fernandina Beach

L ocated in the most northeasterly corner of Florida, Fort Clinch State Park is centered around American military history amid a scenic maritime ecosystem. The park encompasses a peninsula that is surrounded by saltwater on three sides. The two park campgrounds are located in distinctly different environments, giving tent campers a choice of where to stay depending on weather and personal whim.

The Beach Area Camp is located a few hundred feet from the Atlantic Ocean. A boardwalk connects campers to the sea. The 21 campsites are spread along the outside of an open loop. A few palm trees form the only campground vegetation. This area is exposed to the elements—and this can be good or bad depending on the season and weather. In the winter, you may enjoy the warmth of the sun, but the bite of the wind may be too much. That very same wind may be a blessing when the bugs are biting. Summer's heat can melt you out here.

The loop center is occupied by a fully equipped comfort station that has hot showers, flush toilets, and laundry facilities. There is no privacy on this loop and the openness of the large campsites attracts a share of RVs. But if this area doesn't suit you, Fort Clinch offers another camping option.

The River Area Camp is on the other side of the peninsula. It faces out toward the Amelia River, a saltwater estuary that

CAMPGROUND RATINGS

Beauty:	★★★
Site privacy:	★★★
Site spaciousness:	★★★
Quiet:	★★★★
Security:	★★★★★
Cleanliness/upkeep:	★★★★

The restored fort and oceanside recreation make this park a Florida treat.

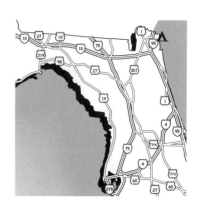

drains the area behind Fort Clinch. A maritime hardwood hammock of live oak, laurel oak, and myrtle oak offer every degree of shade not available in the Beach Camp Area. American holly, yaupon, palmetto, and red cedar form a varied understory.

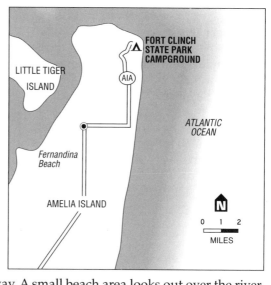

Depending on the wind direction, the River Area Camp can get a few ocean breezes of its own. The 41 campsites are stretched along both sides of the loop road. A few of the sites at the far side of the loop avail an obscured view of the Intercoastal Waterway. A small beach area looks out over the river.

A fully equipped comfort station with the same amenities as at the Beach Area Camp is located toward the river side of the loop. The River Area Camp attracts more tenters and is the preferred camping area. From my point of view, why not camp in the forest and access the beach at your whim?

And Fort Clinch has a great beach. The southern section has high dunes between you and the rest of the mainland. Nearly a mile long, there is ample room for shellers, sunbathers, and surf-fishermen. The extreme northeastern corner of the beach has a pier that extends into the Atlantic. You can also fish the marshy backside of the island.

A short nature trail courses through the hardwood hammock in the center of the park. It is the forested in-between zone as the peninsula makes the transition from beach to marsh.

The highlight of the park is the actual Fort Clinch. Pay $1 to pass through the museum. Look around the museum, then prepare to enter the fort itself. Fort Clinch overlooks the Cumberland Sound. It was occupied by both Confederate and Union forces during the Civil War.

You can climb throughout the fort. Go into the bunkhouses. Look over the stockade. Go to one of the strategic points for fantastic views into the sound, the Atlantic, and the state of Georgia across the water. I felt like a kid running around, climbing staircases, going from one point to the next, checking out the cannons.

I was also lucky enough to witness one of the reenactments held at the fort. On the first full weekend of every month, park rangers come to life as Union forces in the year 1864. Watch them go through the day-to-day chores of a soldier of the area. Families and children get in on the act, too. It really adds to the feel of the fort. Candlelight tours of Fort Clinch are available, but you must make reservations. When you come to Fort Clinch, there will be no acting required to have a good time at this scenic and historic state park.

To **get there** from the town of Fernandina Beach, drive east on A1A for 1 mile. Just before you reach the beach, Fort Clinch State Park will be on your left.

Fort Clinch Campground
2601 Atlantic Avenue
Fernandina Beach, FL 32034

Operated by: Florida State Parks

Information: (904) 277-7274

Open: Year-round

Individual sites: 62

Each site has: Picnic table, fire ring, water, electricity

Site assignment: Assigned by ranger unless specific site asked for

Registration: By phone or at park entrance booth

Facilities: Hot showers, flush toilets, pay phone, laundry, soda machine

Parking: At campsites only

Fee: $13 per night October to February, $19 per night March to September; $2 electricity fee

Elevation: Sea level

Restrictions

Pets—Prohibited

Fires—In fire rings only

Alcoholic beverages—Prohibited

Vehicles—None

Other—14-day stay limit

GOLD HEAD BRANCH CAMPGROUND

Keystone Heights

Rolling hills in Florida? Yeah, that's right. Gold Head Branch is located on what is known as the central ridge of Florida and boasts some serious elevation changes by Sunshine State standards. Steep ravines are cut into these hills, adding more vertical variation. The small campground is located on a hill and rests in flora native to this broken terrain.

Gold Head Branch Campground is divided into two loops. The Sandhill Loop has electrical hookups. Atop a hill, it is in an open area broken by turkey oaks and longleaf pines. Turkey oaks get their name from the tip of the tree's leaf, which resembles a turkey foot. The ground cover consists of sand and wire grass. Wire grass is native to this area and not nearly as bad as it sounds. The 18 campsites encompass only three-quarters of the paved loop. Seven of the campsites are on the inside of the loop.

There may be little campsite privacy, but the sites are very spacious. A comfort station with hot showers is in the loop's center. Some tent campers stay here, but it is mostly RVs in the Sandhill Loop.

The Turkey Oak Loop lacks electricity. It also lacks RVs. It is by far the more appealing of the two loops. The packed-sand road is a bit bumpy as it passes through a shade-giving forest of slash pine, turkey oak, and sand live oak. The understory of wire grass, brush, and young tree seedlings is

CAMPGROUND RATINGS

Beauty:	★★★
Site privacy:	★★★
Site spaciousness:	★★★★
Quiet:	★★★★★
Security:	★★★★★
Cleanliness/upkeep:	★★★★

Camp among the rolling hills and spring-fed lakes of Gold Head Branch State Park.

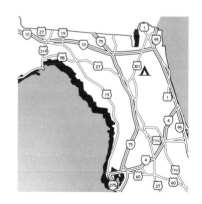

much thicker here, though the woods do thin out toward the end of the loop.

Campsites are very spacious and many offer privacy that is more than adequate. Only four campsites are on the outside of the loop. They back up to an open woodland. The comfort station is on the inside of the loop.

The bumpy dirt road and lack of electricity make Turkey Oak the tent camper's choice. The Lakeview Camping Area has fallen into disrepair and has been closed for several years. Long-term plans for reopening the area are dependent on funding.

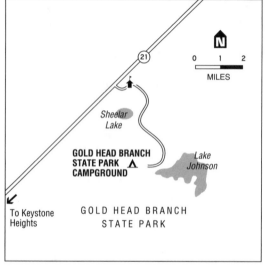

Why do they call it Gold Head anyway? You'll just have to come here to find out. Gold Head Branch is a series of clear springs at the bottom of a steep ravine. This ravine is an inverted island of moisture-loving plants. Water drains out of the sand hills, sinks into the ravine, then comes together to form Gold Head Branch, which flows into Little Lake Johnson.

Follow the boardwalk down to the ravine. Walk the Fern Trail and see the individual springs. You can also walk the Loblolly Trail and see the park's largest loblolly pines. Or walk the Ridge Trail a 1-mile hike that leads down to the old mill site. A man once dammed Gold Head Branch, using its energy to grind corn or gin cotton.

A 3-mile portion of the Florida National Scenic Trail winds through the hills of the park. You'll see open stands of longleaf pine and turkey oak, the natural state of things on the central ridge. This open woodland, punctuated by the wire grass, is maintained by fire. Outside the park, fire is generally suppressed, resulting in the loss of this natural habitat. Start at the entrance station and end near the park cabins.

Old fire roads and the old logging tram road are open to hikers and bikers. These paths crisscross the park. Get a map at the entrance booth so as not to get turned around.

All this hiking can make a body hot. There are five natural lakes in the park. Little Lake Johnson has a swimming beach. Canoes are for rent as well. Big Lake Johnson has a boat ramp and fresh-water fishing. Sheeler Lake is being restored and is closed to fishing and swimming. The other two lakes are Deer Lake and Pebble Lake.

Summer weekends are the only time the campground regularly fills. Winter weekends can be intermittently busy. This is a different and special area, with a campground in an equally unusual setting. The Florida hills are calling you. Can you hear them?

To get there from Keystone Heights, drive north on FL 21 for 6 miles. Gold Head Branch State Park will be on your right.

KEY INFORMATION

Gold Head Branch Campground
6239 State Road 21
Keystone Heights, FL 32356

Operated by: Florida State Parks

Information: (352) 473-4701

Open: Year-round

Individual sites: 18 electric, 19 nonelectric

Each site has: Picnic table, fire ring, water spigot

Site assignment: Assigned by ranger unless specific site asked for

Registration: By phone or at park entrance booth

Facilities: Hot showers, flush toilets, pay phone

Parking: At campsites only

Fee: $10 per night; $2 electricity fee

Elevation: 125 feet

Restrictions

Pets—Prohibited

Fires—In fire rings only

Alcoholic beverages—Prohibited

Vehicles—None

Other—14-day stay limit

LITTLE TALBOT ISLAND CAMPGROUND

Jacksonville

L ittle Talbot Island State Park is one of the area parks collectively known as the Talbot Islands State Parks. In addition to Little Talbot, there is Big Talbot Island, Fort George Island, and Amelia Island State Recreation Area. Little Talbot has a nice 40-unit campground that serves as a well-placed base camp for exploring the beaches, marshlands, and the history of the locale.

The campground is across A1A from the ocean and backs up to a salt marsh. The forest here is fairly thick, a mixture of slash pine, live oak, red cedar, southern magnolia, and palm. An understory of American holly, saw palmetto, and yaupon (another type of holly) provides fine campsite buffers and breaks up the campground. Be aware that the 40 campsites are not uniform in size. Check out the campsites to find a site to suit your dimensional needs.

The campground is divided into three loops of hard, packed sand with a spur road leading to each loop. Campsites are located along the spur roads as well as the loops themselves. There are no campsites on the inside of the loops. The first loop has nine campsites. Most are located on the spur road. A short, dead-end road holds two sites.

The central loop has 13 sites. Most of these are on the spur road, too. The canopy is a little more open here, with more slash pines. Its proximity to the low-lying salt

CAMPGROUND RATINGS

Beauty:	★★★★
Site privacy:	★★★
Site spaciousness:	★★★
Quiet:	★★★
Security:	★★★★★
Cleanliness/upkeep:	★★★★

Little Talbot Island is one of the few barrier islands wholly owned by the state of Florida. Camp here and explore all the nearby coastal state parks.

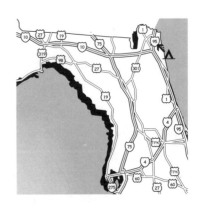

marsh allows more light. A small playground is in the center of this loop.

The third loop has the longest spur road and 17 campsites. The campsites along the spur road are across from an ancient sand dune that is thickly forested. Some of the campsites on the loop open up to the salt marsh and, consequently, have the best view in the campground.

A campground gate keeps the area safe and secure. Two bathhouses are well situated and close to all campers. Both

have hot showers and flush toilets. A pay phone and a washer and dryer are adjacent to the south bathhouse.

Across the road, Little Talbot Island has over 5 miles of pristine beach. Sunbathe, surf-cast or just watch the waves roll in. Don't be surprised to see surfers riding the waves out on North Point. If you are in a walking mood, you can take the Island Hiking Trail to the beach. It starts near the park entrance station and travels through varying maritime plant communities to access the beach at 2.4 miles. Then 1.7 miles of beach-walking will return you the first boardwalk that crosses the dunes back to the main campground road.

The marsh side of the island is worth a look, too. A 1-mile nature trail leaves directly from the campground and skirts the tidal estuary where fishermen are often seen casting for redfish and sea trout. The marsh is also great for crabbing.

Fort George has an informative 4-mile trail of its own. The Saturiwa Trail tells the history of man and the island over the last 5,000 years. You also get to climb Mount Cornelia, the highest coastal point between here and North Carolina. It is an ancient dune that allows views of the mouth of the St. Johns River.

Big Talbot Island is a little more on the quiet side. It is another sea island that offers canoeing, fishing, hiking, and sunbathing. There is a spot known as the Bluffs that sports a view of Nassau Sound. It is a popular photography spot. Nature lovers will really enjoy this island.

Amelia Island is next up the chain of sea islands. The state recreation area is the only undeveloped part of Amelia Island. The highlight here is the opportunity to rent horses and saddle up for a ride along the beach—a very rare opportunity in this day and age.

The Talbot Islands State Parks offer a wide variety of recreational situations. The campground on Little Talbot Island makes an attractive and safe base camp to see the sea islands of northern Florida.

To get there from I-95 in Jacksonville, take FL 105 north (Heckscher Drive) for 22 miles to Little Talbot Island State Park, which will be on your right. Be aware that after 20 miles, SR 105 turns into A1A.

Little Talbot Island Campground
12157 Heckscher Drive
Jacksonville, FL 32226

Operated by: Florida State Parks

Information: (904) 251-2320

Open: Year-round

Individual sites: 40

Each site has: Picnic table, fire ring, water spigot, electricity

Site assignment: Assigned by ranger unless specific site asked for

Registration: By phone or at park entrance booth

Facilities: Hot showers, flush toilets, pay phone, laundry

Parking: At campsites only

Fee: $16 per night March to September, $9 per night October to February; $2 electricity fee

Elevation: Sea level

Restrictions

  Pets—Prohibited

  Fires—In fire rings only

  Alcoholic beverages—Prohibited

  Vehicles—None

  Other—14-day stay limit

MANATEE SPRINGS CAMPGROUND

Chiefland

When the state of Florida began planning state parks, Manatee Springs was one of the first places that came to mind. No wonder—the combination of the historic *Suwannee River*, a huge spring, varied plant communities, and a mammal reserve made Manatee Springs an easy choice. And with a nonelectric camping loop, your choice to come here should be just as easy.

The 100-site campground is divided into three loops. The Magnolia Loop has electrical hookups and the largest sites. This spells RVs. The tall canopy of hardwood has some of the 14 species of oak that thrive in this park, as well as mockernut hickory and butternut hickory. The understory of red bay and palmetto provide some campsite buffers. A children's play area and a fully equipped comfort station center the loop. Sand and leaves cover the Magnolia Loop. Stay here only if the other two loops are full.

The Hickory Loop has electric hookups, too. It is more isolated, with a forest similar to Magnolia Loop, but with a thicker understory of primarily magnolia and red bay. The campsites are along two spur roads that end in small turnaround loops. Stay here if you want to camp with electricity.

The Magnolia Non-electric Loop is the best. There is a mixed forest of evergreen and deciduous trees with the thickest

CAMPGROUND RATINGS

Beauty:	★★★
Site privacy:	★★★
Site spaciousness:	★★★
Quiet:	★★★★
Security:	★★★★★
Cleanliness/upkeep:	★★★★

Manatee Springs is a highlight of the state's Nature Coast.

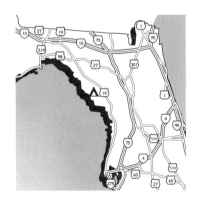

understory of the loops. It is mostly sparkleberry, red bay, and smaller trees. This camping area has an unusual loop-within-a-loop configuration.

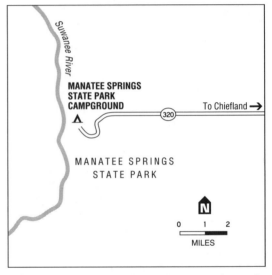

The outer loop has 34 campsites. These sites are each nestled into their own wooded cubbyholes. Some campsites have tent pads; all campsites have a lantern post. Campsite buffers divide the sites, most of which are located on the outside of the loop.

The inner loop has smaller and less-wooded campsites. These seven sites are closest to the bathhouse, though. The Magnolia Non-electric Loop is almost exclusively occupied by tent campers. It is also the most attractive camping area and the one I recommend.

Manatee Springs is impressive. It boils up over 80,000 gallons of clear water per minute. A viewing path lies all around the springhead, where you can look into the water and see lots of fish, turtles, and other aquatic life. Just below the spring's beginning is a roped-off swimming area. Be warned that this swimming area is in the current of Manatee Spring's short but swift flow to the Suwannee River. A calmer pool area has been built across the spring and is accessible by a short foot trail.

Below the swimming area is the canoe launch. Canoes can be rented and you can paddle to the Suwannee. Summer will find tubers floating down the spring and then walking back up time and again via a short boardwalk that meanders through a cypress swamp bordering the spring run.

Viewing platforms have been erected for peering out into the water to look for manatees. At the end of the boardwalk is a dock for boaters, fishermen, and manatee watchers. Here I saw manatees swimming just inside the warmth of the spring run, facing upstream and coming up for air every few minutes.

The North End Trail System is a collection of old fire roads that crisscross the park property for a collective 8.5 miles. These trails pass all manner of forest communities that inhabit this river valley. Both walkers and bicyclers are welcome to enjoy the forest. Turkeys, deer, foxes, and wild boars call this woodland home.

The North End Nature Walk uses some of the trails for an interpretive walk that employs a handheld guide and numbered posts. Learn about plants and trees of this forest and how they interact with each other. Shacklefoot Pond and Graveyard Pond are two worthwhile destinations in the system's southeastern end. Three other trails end near the Suwannee River. Get a map at the Ranger Station so that you don't end up walking in circles.

The great naturalist William Bartram lauded the natural beauty of this area. The state of Florida had Manatee Springs on its short list of initial state parks. Put Manatee Springs on your short list of Florida treasures to come and visit.

To get there from Chiefland, drive west on CR 320 for 6 miles. Manatee Springs State Park will be dead ahead.

KEY INFORMATION

Manatee Springs Campground
11650 N.W. 115 Street
Chiefland, FL 32626

Operated by: Florida State Parks

Information: (352) 493-6072

Open: Year-round

Individual sites: 45 electric, 55 nonelectric

Each site has: Tent pads, fire ring, water

Site assignment: Assigned by ranger unless specific site asked for

Registration: By phone or at park entrance booth

Facilities: Hot showers, flush toilets, pay phone

Parking: At campsites only

Fee: $10 per night; $2 electricity fee

Elevation: 30 feet

Restrictions

Pets—Prohibited

Fires—In fire rings only

Alcoholic beverages—Prohibited

Vehicles—None

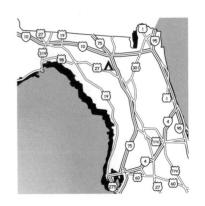

O'LENO CAMPGROUND

High Springs

O'Leno State Park has a strange name derivation. First there was the town of Keno, which was founded near where the Santa Fe River sinks into the limestone below. Keno is a card game of chance, so the town's religious folk decided to rename the town to Leno to save its reputation. Leno soon disappeared after the railroad passed it by. People referred to the area as ol' Leno, thus the name for the park, O'Leno.

The Santa Fe River was the reason for the town and now the river is the reason for the park. The area between the river sink and river rise has been a major crossing point for as long as man has been around. Many who crossed camped in the area; now you can, too. The two park campgrounds, Dogwood and Magnolia, serve tent campers well.

Dogwood Campground is located near the park entrance. A hard, packed-sand road leads into an now-forested sinkhole. The large loop is in a forest of many hardwoods: laurel oak, pignut hickory, and mockernut hickory. Dogwood trees form part of the understory, which also includes many brier patches—nobody wants to walk through them.

The loop rises as it circles around. The 32 campsites are large and well spaced. Brier-free paths lead to the comfort station in the center of the loop. Its distance from the rest of the park makes it the most isolated loop.

CAMPGROUND RATINGS

Beauty:	★★★
Site privacy:	★★★
Site spaciousness:	★★★
Quiet:	★★★
Security:	★★★★★
Cleanliness/upkeep:	★★★★

The unusual Santa Fe River sinks and reappears at O'Leno, one of Florida's oldest state parks.

If the camping is really slow, this loop may be closed.

Magnolia Campground is located on leveler ground. It was built when the park was founded. Loblolly pines tower overhead, along with laurel oak and a few other hardwoods. An understory of red cedar, holly, and, of course, magnolia fill the forest.

The more elongated Magnolia loop has large and open campsites. One small road bisects the loop but has no campsites on it. All 32 sites are on the outside of the loop. A comfort station rests in the loop center.

Both campgrounds are attractive. Magnolia may lure some RVs. Summer weekends are busy for O'Leno. Winter can be very quiet, but is a good time to hike many of the excellent park trails. The Dogwood Trail leads from Dogwood Campground to the Santa Fe River area, center for most of the park's recreation.

The mile-long River Trail crosses the Santa Fe and heads upstream before looping around to circle the river sink, the spot where the river follows subterranean passageways to emerge above ground later. The 1.5-mile River Rise Trail leads from the gate on U.S. 441 and goes to the spot where the Santa Fe emerges from the ground to flow again.

Hikers and bikers can both use the Pareners Branch Loop. It passes its stream namesake and goes by some sinks, areas where the limestone has given way forming a hole in the ground. Part of the trail follows the historic Wire Road that passed this way to cross the Santa Fe where it flowed underground. The Limestone Trail starts on the main park road. It travels by numerous rock outcrops and through a hardwood hammock on its half-mile loop.

The Santa Fe River is popular for swimming. Near the footbridge is a roped-off area with concrete steps leading down to water. Canoes are for rent at the park to explore the scenic river, but fishing is said to be unpredictable.

Many O'Leno campers drive to nearby Ichetucknee Springs State Park. The springs here put forth 233 million gallons of water a day. Tubers love to float its clear water in the summertime. This spring is a National Natural Landmark.

It's hard to believe a town once was here. O'Leno can be a fun family getaway or a quiet off-season retreat. Many have passed this way across the Santa Fe River by way of land. Make sure you pass this way, too.

To get there from High Springs, drive north on U.S. 441 for 6 miles. O'Leno State Park will be on your right.

KEY INFORMATION

O'Leno Campground
Route 2, Box 1010
High Springs, FL 32643

Operated by: Florida State Parks

Information: (904) 454-1853

Open: Year-round

Individual sites: 64

Each site has: Picnic table, fire ring, water, electricity

Site assignment: Assigned by ranger unless specific site asked for

Registration: By phone or at park entrance booth

Facilities: Hot showers, flush toilets

Parking: At campsites only

Fee: $11 per night; $2 electricity fee

Elevation: 70 feet

Restrictions

Pets—Prohibited

Fires—In fire rings only

Alcoholic beverages—Prohibited

Vehicles—None

Other—14-day stay limit

OCEAN POND CAMPGROUND

Lake City

Ocean Pond is a misleading name for the body of water by this campground. Neither ocean nor pond, it is a bowl-shaped lake 2 miles in diameter. However, it is not misleading to call this Forest Service recreation area scenic and worth a visit.

The campground is spread along the shore of Ocean Pond. Tall pines tower overhead. Spanish moss hangs from the hardwoods. A dense understory of palmetto and young oak thrives where it hasn't been cut back. Grass and pine needles carpet the forest edges. Cypress trees border Ocean Pond.

Just beyond the registration board are the only two marginal sites. They are open and too close to the road. Just beyond these two sites, the main campground road divides. To the right is a large loop containing only seven sites. The campground host shares this loop, which is set back from the lake. These sites are very roomy and relaxed, seeming like a minicampground of its own. A bathhouse with hot shower serves this loop.

To the left is the bulk of the campground. A sandy road stretches along the shore. Six of the coveted lakeside sites are on one side of the road. Here, you can float your boat right up to the campsite. Across from the main road is a spur road containing five large sites by a comfort station.

Farther on is a miniloop containing three more lakeside sites. These sites are large as

CAMPGROUND RATINGS

Beauty:	★★★★
Site privacy:	★★★★
Site spaciousness:	★★★★
Quiet:	★★
Security:	★★★
Cleanliness/upkeep:	★★★★

Ocean Pond Campground is the pride of the Oseola National Forest.

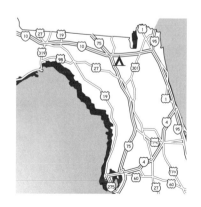

---

well, with their own comfort station. A final loop contains the 20 remaining sites. Five open sites and a comfort station occupy the interior of the loop. Three more sites are directly lakeside. The rest are cut into the thick woods, offering the maximum in site privacy, though they may be a bit buggy on a still summer day.

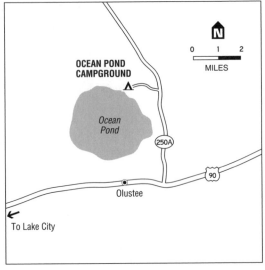

Overall, the campsites are among the largest I've ever seen. Plenty of brush provides more than ample site privacy, though the lakeside sites are more open. Water spigots are spread throughout the campground. Unfortunately, a few RVs will be spread there, too. Another drawback is that the wind blows the wrong way, you can sometimes hear traffic from I-10.

Ocean Pond attracts a cross section of campers who enjoy a cross section of activities. It is full on summer weekends and holidays but maintains a pleasant atmosphere. The ultimate testimony comes from the campground host. He and his wife have stayed here for the past three years.

A boat ramp serves the campground, allowing boaters to fish for largemouth bass, bluegill, or crappie. Ocean Pond is big enough to enjoy other water sports, too. Both kids and adults can enjoy the campground swimming beach. Near the beach is a grassy glade ideal for sunbathing, throwing a Frisbee or just relaxing on the lakefront benches.

Ocean Pond is lucky enough to be in the path of the state's most famous walkway, the Florida National Scenic Trail. A 22-mile stretch of the trail winds northwest through the Osceola, from Olustee Battlefield to U.S. 441. You can traverse one of the more than 20 boardwalks that span swamps and other wetlands of the north Florida flatwoods.

The Olustee Battlefield is just a short drive or a longer walk from Ocean Pond. Here is the site of the battle of Olustee, the largest Civil War battle fought in Florida. Explore the small museum there.

Numerous lakes, creeks, and ponds are sprinkled about the Osceola. But the most interesting feature may be the 13,600-acre Big Gum Swamp Wilderness. The water table is generally near the surface, creating a spongy mat that may or may not hold you up. Piney woods and sluggish creeks add to the terrain. One trail, the Silver Dot, starts near Forest Road 262. The adventurous can follow old elevated tramways, remnants of "turpentining" operations of the late 1800s. Be sure to stop at the Osceola District Office between Lake City and Ocean Pond for a detailed map.

No matter where you go in the Osceola National Forest, make Ocean Pond your base camp. It is an appealing campground in a diverse national forest.

To get there from Lake City, drive east on U.S. 90 for 14 miles. Turn left at CR 250-A just beyond the town of Olustee. Follow CR 250-A for 4 miles and turn left into the campground entrance.

KEY INFORMATION

Ocean Pond Campground
U.S. Highway 90 East
P.O. Box 70
Olustee, FL 32072

Operated by: U.S. Forest Service

Information: (904) 942-9351

Open: Year-round

Individual sites: 50

Each site has: Tent pad, picnic table, fire ring, lantern post

Site assignment: First come, first served; no reservations

Registration: Self-registration on site

Facilities: Hot showers, flush toilets, pay phone

Parking: At campsites only

Fee: $8 per night

Elevation: 160 feet

Restrictions

  Pets—On leash only

  Fires—In fire rings only

  Alcoholic beverages—Prohibited

  Vehicles—None

  Other—14-day stay limit

PAYNES PRAIRIE CAMPGROUND

Gainesville

A buffalo on a prairie was about the last thing I expected to see in Florida. But there it was. After perusing the area, I understood why Florida called Paynes Prairie a preserve. Over 20,000 acres of water and land support bird, reptile, and mammalian wildlife. The well-arranged tent-only area made Paynes Prairie complete.

Well, it's not a prairie in the midwestern sense but rather a basin of grassy marshland surrounded by forest. The vegetation growing on the prairie gives a sense of endless grassland. The grass and forest are constantly giving and taking as water rises and lowers. It is a story of nature that has to be seen to be appreciated.

Tent campers can surely appreciate the Puc Puggy Campground. It is in a mixed forest of pine, laurel oak, and hardwoods such as maple. Younger hardwood seedlings and some palmetto form an adequate understory. Magnolia and holly are also present. The woods are certainly pleasing to the eye.

The campground is arranged in a loop. The first 20 campsites are for all types of campers and some sites have built-in tent pads. Just beyond the foot trail to Lake Wauberg, the Tent Camping Area begins. Four parking areas are there for tent campers to pull in. Then it is a short walk to their sites, nestled in the woods. Electrical hookups are randomly spread about the tent area. Not all tenters can access these

CAMPGROUND RATINGS

Beauty:	★★★
Site privacy:	★★★★
Site spaciousness:	★★★
Quiet:	★★
Security:	★★★★★
Cleanliness/upkeep:	★★★★

Wild horses, buffalo, and a prairie in Florida? It's all here in Paynes Prairie, with an area for tent campers only!

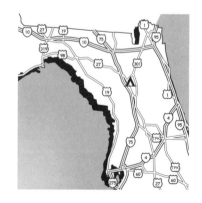

---

plugs, unless they bring a very long extension cord.

Campsites 21 through 24 have their own little walking loop. They are closest to Lake Wauberg but don't access it. The next three sites have their own loop. One of the campsites is close to the road, the other two are back 30 to 40 yards. These sites have the best privacy, though all the tent-camping sites have ample privacy and spaciousness.

The next eight campsites are mostly back off the road and are connected to two parking

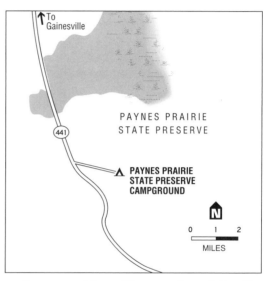

areas by paths. Pine needles cover the ground here. The woods and the distance from the road make for a wonderful tent-camping experience. The only drawback is the low hum of autos from I-75 a few miles away.

The main camping loop continues with 17 sites. These campsites are all appealing and attractive, but the tent sites are the only way to go at Paynes Prairie. Two bathhouses serve the campground. They both have hot showers and flush toilets. Oddly enough, if the campground goes below 50% capacity, then the rangers shut down the south bathhouse, the one by the tent campers. This was the case during my trip here.

That was the only drawback of any sort. I methodically explored this large preserve. First, I watched the 20-minute video in the Visitor Center to grasp an overall perspective. I highly recommend the video. There are places it shows that you simply can't access by trail.

Then I climbed the observation tower overlooking the prairie. I spotted two of the wild horses and a buffalo. I returned to camp after watching the sun set over Lake Wauberg. Back at my campsite I perused the preserve map for the next day's hiking opportunities.

There are plenty. Cone's Dike is an 8-mile round-trip jaunt that heads into the marsh. Chacala is a series of loops that start near the campground encompassing varied terrain, eventually reaching Chacala Pond. Both of these trails are for hikers and bikers. Bolen's Bluff Trail starts off U.S. 441, travels 1.5 miles into the marsh, and ends at a wildlife viewing deck. The 17-mile Gainesville-Hawthorne Trail is a rails-to-trails project that is open to horses as well as hikers and bikers.

Lake Wauberg makes an ideal canoeing destination, whether you are fishing or not. Gas-powered engines are prohibited, making for a quiet paddling experience. Keep an eye open for alligators. Nearby Gainesville offers the eclectic atmosphere of a university town. Watch for Gators here, too.

Humans have been a presence on the prairie for thousands of years. Thankfully, the state is restoring and making Paynes Prairie available for both wildlife and humans to range and roam upon. You have got to see it to truly appreciate it.

To get there from Gainesville, drive south on U.S. 441 for about 10 miles. Paynes Prairie State Preserve will be on your left.

KEY INFORMATION

Paynes Prairie Campground
Route 2, Box 41
Micanopy, FL 32667-9702

Operated by: Florida State Parks

Information: (352) 466-3397

Open: Year-round

Individual sites: 15 tent only, 42 tent and trailer

Each site has: Picnic table, fire ring, water, lantern post; some have electricity

Site assignment: Assigned by ranger unless specific site asked for

Registration: By phone or at park entrance booth

Facilities: Hot showers, flush toilets

Parking: At campsites and overflow parking

Fee: $10 per night; $2 electricity fee

Elevation: 75 feet

Restrictions

Pets—Prohibited

Fires—In fire rings only

Alcoholic beverages—Prohibited

Vehicles—None

SUWANNEE RIVER CAMPGROUND

Live Oak

This park is a good example of a state protecting, developing, and preserving a special area for present and future generations to enjoy. At this site, the town of Columbus once saw steamboats coming and going along the Suwannee River. The city eventually was abandoned. This important river crossing was protected by Confederate soldiers; you can still see their earthworks. Today, forest has reclaimed the area. The rivers are justly important for their scenic value, as they have always been. The state of Florida rightly saw fit to make this one of its first state parks.

The Suwannacoochee Camp Area is located on a high area back from the Suwannee River. Follow the sand road through the campground. Above, tall laurel oak, live oak, and longleaf pines shade the area. There are campsites on both sides of the loop. The sites are large and well separated from one another but have a moderate understory of younger hardwoods.

The campground road turns left just before coming to the historic stagecoach road that once ran through Columbus. The forest floor is thick with oak leaves and pine needles. As the campground road turns away from the stagecoach road, all the campsites are on the inside of the loop. Holly trees and vines complement the understory. Across from these sites is a field, which offers more light than the

CAMPGROUND RATINGS

Beauty:	★★★
Site privacy:	★★★
Site spaciousness:	★★★★
Quiet:	★★★★
Security:	★★★★
Cleanliness/upkeep:	★★★★

Camp in wooded uplands where the Withlacoochee and Suwannee rivers meet in an historic setting.

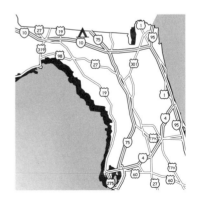

---

forested area. It may be a good idea to camp at these sites on a dark day.

As the campground road makes its final turn, two more campsites appear on the outside of the loop. These sites are the largest in the campground.

A fully equipped comfort station with hot showers and flush toilets is in the loop's center. It also has a washer and dryer for those dirty duds. Each campsite has posts embedded into its perimeter, marking the sites off and adding some decorative landscaping.

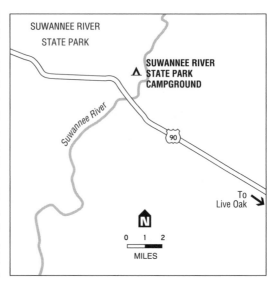

The 31-site campground has aged well. Its only drawback is that every campsite has electrical hookups, which could result in an RV for a neighbor. The warm season sees mostly tent campers. Weekends are infrequently full, and weekdays are quiet year-round. Sometimes it's so quiet it becomes hard to imagine the town of Columbus ever being here. Suwannee River does see a fair share of travelers looking for a place to stay for the night because of its proximity to I-10 and I-75. However, on my weekday visit, I was the only camper other than the campground host.

The Suwannee River was running even darker than normal—it was above flood stage. The Timucuan Indian word *Suwannee* means "black water." A light drizzle fell and the dark sky made spring's brilliant greenery even more vivid as I hiked the series of nature trails near the campground.

I started with the Suwannee River Trail that ran along the flowing watercourse. Two other trails spur off this one. The Balanced Rock Trail heads upstream for a half-mile to the Balanced Rock and connects to the Lime Sink Run Trail. It follows up a stream branch to a spring and leads back to the campground.

There are many springs along the Suwannee and Withlacoochee Rivers. The Earthworks Trail passes by the old mill site and the Confederate earthworks that once protected the bridge spanning the Suwannee. This trail ends at an overlook where you can see the Suwannacoochee Springs. The name reflects the confluence of the Suwannee and Withlacoochee Rivers.

The Sandhills Trail makes a three-quarter-mile loop through an open, drier environment and passes the Columbus Cemetery. A fairly recent acquisition of land across the Suwannee has an 11-mile loop trail for hardy hikers that parallels the Withlacoochee River. This trail intersects the famed Florida National Scenic Trail.

Most people rightly associate the park with canoeing. The Suwannee is Florida's greatest river. It's even mentioned in the state song. The springs and scenery have captured many a paddler's heart as they passed this way. The Withlacoochee River is characterized by high limestone banks and many cypress and tupelo trees. The beautiful pool of Blue Spring is just below the put-in for a canoe run that ends at the state park. Both rivers make for many miles of scenic river floating.

Suwannee River State Park has a good campground. It has better nature trails. And it has Florida's greatest river. It makes for a good stopover if you are just passing through but also makes a fine destination in and of itself. The state was right for making Suwannee River one of its first state parks.

To get there from Live Oak, take U.S. 90 west for 11 miles. Suwannee River State Park will be on your right.

KEY INFORMATION

Suwannee River Campground
Route 8, Box 297
Live Oak, FL 32060

Operated by: Florida State Parks

Information: (904) 362-2746

Open: Year-round

Individual sites: 31

Each site has: Picnic table, fire ring, water, electricity

Site assignment: First come, first served; no reservations

Registration: At Ranger Station at 5 P.M.

Facilities: Hot showers, flush toilets, pay phone, laundry

Parking: At campsites and extra car parking

Fee: $10 per night March to September, $8 per night October to February; $2 electricity fee

Elevation: 50 feet

Restrictions

Pets—Prohibited

Fires—In fire

Alcoholic beverages—Prohibited

Vehicles—None

Other—14-day stay limit

CENTRAL
FLORIDA

CENTRAL FLORIDA

ALEXANDER SPRINGS CAMPGROUND

Umatilla

Alexander Springs is clearly worth preserving, an oasis in the forest, one of the outstanding physical features of central Florida. Imagine thrashing through broken woods and coming upon this upwelling of clear-blue water rising out of the earth and instantaneously forming its own waterway. This is Alexander Springs.

The U.S. Forest Service recognized this aquatic wonder and built a fine recreation area around the spring. It's showing signs of age, but any man-made facility will fail to match the natural ones here. Native Timucuan Indians recognized the beauty of the springs. Their artifacts make it evident they called it home. Now you can make the springs your home for a night or two weeks.

The campground is split into four spur roads that turn away from, then return to, the main campground road. The campground rises as it extends away from the springs. Loop A is on the highest ground, in a forest of pines with an adequate understory of palmetto. This 14-campsite loop has a central comfort station with flush toilets only. During the winter months Loop A is where the RV-driving "snowbirds" congregate.

Loop B spurs off to the right of the main campground road. It is more thickly forested with live oak and has a more swampy appearance, being on lower, wetter ground. Warm-water showers and flush toilets are at the center of this loop in the

CAMPGROUND RATINGS

Beauty:	★★★★
Site privacy:	★★★
Site spaciousness:	★★★★
Quiet:	★★★
Security:	★★★★
Cleanliness/upkeep:	★★★

First Timucuan Indians, then Florida pioneers, and now you can enjoy Alexander Springs.

comfort station. This comfort station houses the only showers actually in the campground. The only other showers are located at the comfort station by the springs. The campground host resides in this loop.

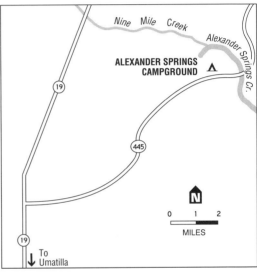

Loop C is on the high side of the campground. It is in a forest of pine, except where the spur road comes back to the main road in a stand of live oaks. Palmetto and small trees form campsite buffers. This 17-site loop also has a central comfort station.

Loop D is at the end of the campground road and is my favorite. Live oaks drape their limbs over the campsites, providing ample shade. Palmetto and hardwood seedlings separate the sites from one another. Being in the rear of the campground, this loop receives the least amount of incidental traffic.

Generous room is given to all campsites. Time has allowed vegetation to provide site buffers throughout the campground, breaking it up and enhancing everyone's camping experience. There is no eyesore trash here, only natural beauty.

The first thing to do is explore the springs. A picnic area leads to a swimming beach adjacent to the springs. Swimmers, snorkelers, scuba divers, and sunbathers congregate at the spot where the clear water rises from the ground and then forms its own river.

This is where the Alexander Springs Creek canoe run begins. Rent a canoe and paddle the wide, sun-splashed waterway. The current is moderate enough for you to return upstream to conclude your paddle. Or you can paddle downstream to one of three landings and arrange a shuttle ride with the on-site park concessionaire. You might want to bring your pole and try to catch some fish.

For land lovers, there is the interesting 1-mile interpretive Timucuan Indian Trail. It runs near Alexander Springs and points out native plants that were used by the Indians in their everyday lives. The trail forms a loop and returns to the picnic area. A spur trail starts near the entrance booth and leads a short distance to the Florida National Scenic Trail. No matter whether you head east or west, you will see a fast-disappearing real Florida.

Hard-core natural enthusiasts will want to explore the Billies Bay Wilderness, which surrounds Alexander Springs on three sides. The centerpiece of this wilderness is Nine Mile Creek. Make sure to talk to a ranger or an experienced local before you delve into this primitive section of the Ocala National Forest.

Alexander Springs is a year-round attraction and will be busy on summer and winter weekends. So whether you come here to cool off from the heat or cool down from the stresses of everyday life, your needs will be met. This surge of water has been enjoyed for thousands of years by all who have discovered its beauty. Make your discovery of Alexander Springs.

To get there from Umatilla, go north on State Hwy. 19 for 8 miles. Turn right on CR 445 and drive 5 miles. Alexander Springs Recreation Area will be on your left.

KEY INFORMATION

Alexander Springs Campground
10863 East Highway 40
Silver Springs, FL 34488

Operated by: U.S. Forest Service

Information: 352-625-2520

Open: Year-round

Individual sites: 67

Each site has: Picnic table, fire ring, lantern post

Site assignment: First come, first served; no reservations

Registration: At campground entrance booth

Facilities: Warm showers, flush toilets, water spigots, pay phone

Parking: At campsites only

Fee: $10 per night

Elevation: 55 feet

Restrictions

   Pets—On 6-foot leash only

   Fires—In fire rings only

   Alcoholic beverages—At campsites only

   Vehicles—None

   Other—14-day stay limit

CENTRAL FLORIDA

BLUE SPRING CAMPGROUND

Orange City

Every winter, manatees leave the cooling waters of the St. Johns River to make the 72° F waters of Blue Spring their home. Now this park has become famous as a place to observe the gentle creature. In the summer, human creatures flock to the spring to swim in the waters and escape the heat. As a result, the park and the campground stay fairly busy year-round.

The campground is situated atop a sandy hill in a sand-scrub thicket. A hard, packed-sand road forms a large loop with a smaller inner loop. Throughout the campground, the understory of wax myrtle and laurel oak, along with other bushes, forms dense camp-site buffers, availing the maximum in site privacy but little overhead protection from the sun.

The campsites are bright and open. Approximately half of the campsites are equipped with electricity, attracting some drive-in campers. But the electric sites are grouped together for the most part, putting like-minded campers together; however, there are no official tent-only sections in which to camp.

The first four sites in the main loop are very open and nonelectric. Then begins a string of 14 electric sites, all on the outside of the loop. As the main loop makes a **U**-turn, a grouping of 20 nonelectric sites begins. A tree canopy forms in places here, allowing some shade.

CAMPGROUND RATINGS

Beauty: ★★★
Site privacy: ★★★★★
Site spaciousness: ★★★
Quiet: ★★
Security: ★★★★★
Cleanliness/upkeep: ★★★★

Come see the winter home of Florida's endangered water mammal, the manatee.

Just past this group of camp-sites, the inner loop begins. It has six electric sites. This inner loop is closer to either of the comfort stations, both of which have hot showers and flush toilets for each sex. Returning to the main loop, a last grouping of seven electric sites brings you to the beginning of the campground.

The lack of shade may sound unappealing, but this campground is unusual for Florida. There is a hint of hilliness to it, and the dense brush between campsites is a plus for campers who value their privacy. Most

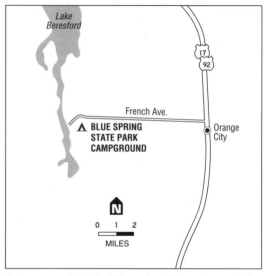

sites have enough growth around them to shield all but the direct rays of the noontime sun from their campsites.

On my trip to Blue Spring, I walked straight from the campground to the boardwalk that meanders the length of the spring from its wellhead to its confluence with the St. Johns River. I entered the shady hammock and looked out on the clear water as it flowed by. Passing the entrance point for scuba divers, I sought the springs "boil." The area has been restored from earlier days when swimmers destroyed the springside vegetation.

There it was, the blue hole for which the area was named. Divers can reach 120 feet into the spring before the force of the spring's upwelling turns them back. Following the flow back downstream, I came to the primary observation deck. The waters revealed a plethora of fish below me: bass, bream, catfish, and long-nose gar.

Across the flow from the deck I spotted it—a manatee! It was facing upstream, rising every few minutes to get a breath of air. Later I saw a mother and calf, gliding upstream toward the springhead. This area is off limits to all boats and serves as a protective zone for some of the approximately 85 manatees of the St. Johns River system.

Turning around, I looked over the Thursby House—built on a mound of snail shells! Snails were the primary food for the Indians of this region, and they left piles of shells as testimony to the importance of this food in their diet. This three-story house was once the center of activity in the early days of orange cultivation in central Florida.

Boaters have access to the ramp near the Thursby House, and canoes are for rent, too. Fishing in the St. Johns is said to be good. You can see for yourself that there are fish in the vicinity. Perhaps the best way to enjoy the water is to take a two-hour ecotour of the St. Johns. Tour boats depart twice daily; riding above you can see the wildlife of the river system below.

Hikers can take their own ecotour of the park on the 4-mile Backwoods Trail. It takes you through hardwood hammocks, marsh, cypress swamp, and pine flatwoods. Give yourself enough time to return as this trail is a one-way trip.

No matter what the season, Blue Spring has something to offer. The springs keep the endangered manatee warm in the winter and you cool in the summer. Don't pass this central Florida attraction by for that other one in Orlando.

To get there from U.S. 17/92 in Orange City, drive 2 miles west on French Avenue to Blue Spring State Park, which will be on your left.

KEY INFORMATION

Blue Spring Campground
2100 West French Avenue
Orange City, FL 32763

Operated by: Florida State Parks

Information: (904) 775-3663

Open: Year-round

Individual sites: 51

Each site has: Picnic table, fire grate, water; 28 sites have electricity

Site assignment: Assigned by ranger unless specific site asked for

Registration: By phone or at park entrance booth

Facilities: Hot showers, flush toilets, pay phone, camp store

Parking: At campsites only

Fee: $16 per night nonelectric; $2 electricity fee

Elevation: 35 feet

Restrictions

Pets—Prohibited

Fires—In fire grates only

Alcoholic beverages—Prohibited

Vehicles—None

Other—None

HILLSBOROUGH RIVER CAMPGROUND

Zephyrhills

Hillsborough River State Park has been providing tent campers with a fun and scenic destination for generations. The river here has some actual rapids, where the water flows over limestone creating those white-water sounds associated with more hilly environments. This was also a strategic spot for a river crossing during the Seminole Wars; the U.S. Army established a fort here in the 1830s. Nearly a century later, the state of Florida established a state park here for your enjoyment.

The campground is divided into two loops, Hammock and River's Edge. The Hammock Loop has 32 electric sites. A forest of large live oak and mature pine make for a dense forest canopy. A thin understory of palmetto divides the mostly open sites that primarily attract RVs.

The Hammock Loop is attractive in its own right. A comfort station with hot showers, flush toilets, laundry, and sinks for washing dishes is in the center of the loop. The sites close to the comfort station are more open.

The River's Edge Loop contains 82 campsites. But it is really divided into two loops of its own. The right-hand loop has 49 all-electric sites beneath a forest much like the Hammock Loop except with more palm trees. The center of the loop is an open grassy field with a play area for kids. A fully equipped comfort station is on the far side of the loop as you enter. The best

CAMPGROUND RATINGS

Beauty:	★★★
Site privacy:	★★★
Site spaciousness:	★★★
Quiet:	★★★
Security:	★★★★★
Cleanliness/upkeep:	★★★★

The scenic Hillsborough River and historic Fort Foster are the highlights of one of Florida's oldest state parks.

To
Zephyrhills

HILLSBOROUGH RIVER
STATE PARK
CAMPGROUND

sites of this area are the seven campsites that back up to the river. The electricity is going to make this area more RV oriented, especially in the winter when the "snowbirds" make their appearance.

The left-hand loop contains 29 nonelectric campsites, the exceptions being the first four, which are electric. There are more pines in this loop and the palmetto understory is much thicker, allowing better campsite privacy for the campers, almost all of which are tent campers. The campsites get bigger as you continue along the loop.

A fully equipped comfort station, minus laundry facilities, is in this loop. Campsites are spread along both sides of the road but provide the most privacy in the entire campground. Tent campers will want to stay in this loop.

A series of nature trails follow the river, informing you about the native flora of the region. They leave from the picnic area and connect to the short Rapids Trail. Two bridges span the Hillsborough River and lead to more hiking opportunities. You can cross either the suspension bridge or the stationary bridge to access the Baynard Nature Trail, which explores the hardwood hammock of the river floodplain. The trail was named for a previous superintendent of the park.

The Hillsborough River Hiking Trail makes a 3.3-mile loop across the river. It parallels the watercourse, then veers back northeast, crossing several boardwalks through cypress swamps. Cross the stationary bridge and turn left to begin this trail. The Wetlands Trail makes a round-trip 3-mile hike through an area being restored to its natural wetlands environment. It is for both bikers and hikers.

Canoeing the Hillsborough is always fun. Canoes are for rent on site and you can fish for bass, bream, or catfish. Watch out for those rapids. No swimming is allowed in the river, though, there is a large swimming pool that is open during warmer months.

On weekends, guided tours of Fort Foster are conducted. Self-guided tours are the only way to go during the week. Either way, you will see the reconstructed fort and the bridge it protected. You can gain insight into the way of life for a soldier in the 1830s, fighting in the Second Seminole War.

Nowadays, you may have to battle a few campers for space on winter weekends. Make a reservation to be sure of a site. After the first of April, things slow down. Summer weekdays are quiet, but swimmers will come here on weekends. Fall can be a good time to canoe the river. Get your supplies in nearby Zephyrhills and get to camping at Hillsborough River State Park.

> **T**o get there from Zephyrhills, drive south on U.S. 301 for 6 miles. Hillsborough River State Park will be on your right.

KEY INFORMATION

Hillsborough River Campground
15402 U.S. 301 North
Thonotosassa, FL 33592

Operated by: Florida State Parks

Information: (813) 987-6771

Open: Year-round

Individual sites: 90 electric, 24 nonelectric

Each site has: Picnic table, fire ring, water spigot

Site assignment: Assigned by ranger unless specific site asked for

Registration: By phone or at park entrance booth

Facilities: Hot shower, flush toilets, pay phone, laundry

Parking: At campsites and extra car parking

Fee: $15 per night; $2 electricity fee

Elevation: 45 feet

Restrictions

Pets—Prohibited

Fires—In fire rings only

Alcoholic beverages—Prohibited

Vehicles—None

Other—14-day stay limit

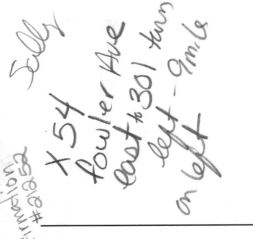

HOG ISLAND CAMPGROUND

Brooksville

Hog Island Campground is situated along the dark and alluring Withlacoochee River. Within the confines of the Withlacoochee State Forest, Hog Island enjoys the beauty of the surrounding woodland in addition to the serpentine Withlacoochee River, a designated Florida State Canoe Trail. Though holidays and weekends bring their fair share of visitors, Hog Island retains that quiet and relaxed atmosphere that tent campers long to enjoy.

The campground is actually across the river from Hog Island. A packed-sand road divides the thick riverside forest, forming a teardrop-shaped loop that circles the campground. Live oak, hickory, and maple trees, draped in Spanish moss, keep the campground shaded. Palmetto and smaller trees form a dense understory dividing the well-dispersed sites. Squirrels scamper about the campground as if they own it.

There are no sites abutting the Withlacoochee that are open to car campers; however, there is a special riverside campsite reserved for canoe campers making their way downstream. Southern cypress trees, with their oxygen-seeking knots, line the river as it encircles Hog Island.

The first few sites at the beginning of the loop are more open. Campsites are situated both inside and outside the loop. As you near the river, the campsites become more frequented, but no sites look worn for wear.

CAMPGROUND RATINGS

Beauty: ★★★★
Site privacy: ★★★★
Site spaciousness: ★★★★★
Quiet: ★★★
Security: ★★
Cleanliness/upkeep: ★★★

Hog Island is a tent camper's hog heaven!

After passing the riverbank picnic area, the loop passes the
bathhouse. The bathhouse is
lighted and has electrical out-
lets near the sinks. Flush toilets
and hot showers complete the
ensemble.

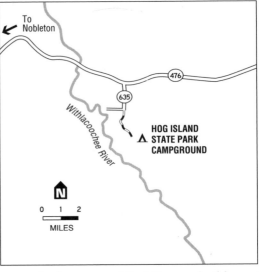

The best campsites are those
on the loop beyond the bathhouse. Sawn logs form campground stools at each site. The
sandy campground floor is
carpeted with fallen leaves
from the hardwood forest. I've
never seen sites so widely scattered. Thirsty campers will be
relieved to know that each
campsite has its own spigot. However, be forewarned that the one bathhouse
will be a walk for those on the far side of this sizable loop.

But what is a little walk in this beautiful place? There are two trails directly
accessible from the campground. The Hog Island Nature Trail weaves through
the riverine woods making a 1.75-mile loop. I hiked the path in the early morning hours, spotting three deer, while following the numbered posts explaining
the various components of the Withlacoochee basin ecosystems.

Hog Island is part of the Croom Unit of the Withlacoochee State Forest. Just
before the campground loop, a trail runs roughly parallel to the river south for
6.8 miles to Silver Lake. Silver Lake is basically a wide spot in the
Withlacoochee, just below the confluence of the Withlacoochee and Little
Withlacoochee Rivers.

In addition to these trails, there are 25 more miles of hiking to enjoy in the
Croom Unit. These trails meander through a host of environments, from live
oak thickets to pine stands to open prairie lands, as well as through signs of
human habitation, old homesites, and abandoned mines.

If you want to enjoy the Withlacoochee River, take a canoe. There is a boat launch right next to the campground. There are two more launches upstream at Iron Bridge and Silver Lake. If you are boatless, several outfitters in nearby Nobleton, just downstream on County Road 476, will be happy to rent you a canoe. Convenient but costly supplies can be purchased here, too. A quiet float downriver is an ideal way to observe wildlife. Fishing for largemouth bass and panfish can be good. The scenery is guaranteed.

There are no bad sites in this intimate campground. But don't expect everything to be perfect here; it's managed by the financially strapped Florida Division of Forestry. Yet they do the best they can with available resources. And with the lush woodland and scenic river, they had fine natural resources with which to start.

To get there from Nobleton, drive east on CR 476. Then turn right on CR 635 and drive 1 mile to a 4-way intersection. Continue forward on the dirt road for 300 yards and Hog Island Campground will be on your right.

Hog Island Campground
15019 Broad Street
Brooksville, FL 34601

Operated by: Florida Division of Forestry 352-754-6896

Information: ~~(904) 754-6777~~

Open: Year-round 352-540-6061

Individual sites: 20

Each site has: Picnic table, fire ring, water spigot

Site assignment: First come, first served; no reservations

Registration: Self-registration, on site

Facilities: Hot showers, flush toilets, pay phone

Parking: At campsites only

Fee: $12 per night

Elevation: 90 feet

Restrictions

Pets—Prohibited

Fires—In fire rings only

Alcoholic beverages—Prohibited

Vehicles—One vehicle per campsite

Other—14-day stay limit

HONTOON ISLAND CAMPGROUND

Deland

L eave the bustling world behind as you cross the St. Johns River and enter the natural and seemingly remote world of Hontoon Island. The campground here is simply fantastic, and there is plenty of human and natural history to keep you thanking the state of Florida for preserving such a gem.

Carry all your necessary camping gear to the free park ferry. It runs from 8 A.M. until sunset. Stand on the dock and somebody from the park will be right over. The five-minute crossing of the St. Johns brings you to the park marina. Unload your gear and register to camp. Don't worry about being assigned a campsite; they are all good. After registering, load your gear in the park van for the quarter-mile ride to the campground.

The 12-site campground is in a loop that is shared with some rustic cabins. The park van will drop you off at your particular campsite. Unload your gear and begin to enjoy. The whole process from car to camp takes less than 30 minutes.

The campground is in a beautiful grove of longleaf pines, sabal palms, and live oak. Each tree shoots upward in competition for sunlight. Pine and oak duff litter the camp-ground floor like a natural carpet. A scatter-ing of the ever-present palmetto and short sabal palms completes the flora ensemble.

The campsites start on the left-hand side of the loop. The first seven campsites are

CAMPGROUND RATINGS

Beauty:	★★★★★
Site privacy:	★★★
Site spaciousness:	★★★★★
Quiet:	★★★
Security:	★★★★★
Cleanliness/upkeep:	★★★★★

A short ferry ride will deliver you to central Florida's best tent camping.

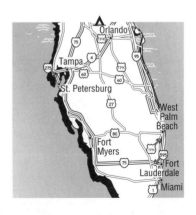

on the loop's interior near the clean comfort station, fully equipped with hot showers, flush toilets, and an electrical outlet for plug-in toiletries. Water spigots are located throughout the intimate campground.

Campsites 8 through 11 continue on the outside of the loop near the beginning of the Timucuan Trail Road. Campsite 12 sits all by itself inside the continuation of the loop. As with all the campsites, it has space for more gear than you can tote on the ferry. The

trunks of the forest grove and some brush allow for enough site privacy, but it is unlikely to be very crowded here.

Winter is the busiest season at Hontoon Island, but even then it's not that busy. The campground may fill on a few holiday weekends. In the summer, the heat and potential for bug problems keep most campers away.

But I say go for it, no matter what time of the year. The park has a really laid-back feel and the rangers can become your friends in one visit—probably because they don't have to deal with hordes of tourists asking inane questions like, "Where is the bathroom?" and "Where is the pop machine?" Speaking of which, there is a tiny camp store on the island with "pop," ice, and a few other items.

You probably won't even want to leave this campground, but just in case you get the itch to wander, there are things to see and do. First, walk back toward the landing and climb the 80-foot observation tower. Get a lay of the land, er, water. The Hammock Hiking Nature Trail is a must. It wanders on boardwalks and land through the forest primeval and ends at an old Indian shell mound. The Timucuans found this place way before we did. Allow two hours of hiking time. Old fire roads thread the island and make ideal walks or bike rides, but you must bring your own bicycle.

The Timucuan Trail extends the length of the island and forms the backbone of the paths. It passes through open pine woods that have been maintained by fire, just as it happened before the white man came. The River to River Road spans the breadth of the island and connects to the Hammock Nature Trail, making loop-hiking possibilities.

Toward dusk, I walked up the Rabbit Run Road. It intersects other roads and has two riverside end points. A rain shower had fallen earlier. The sky had cleared and a mist rose from the palmetto while the sun set over the open, park-like pine woods. As I turned the corner, two white-tailed deer froze in their tracks, then scampered off into the brush. I returned to camp.

Canoes are for rent at the park. You can explore the St. Johns sloughs and currents, as well as the Hontoon Dead River, where the flow of the St. Johns changed course in times previous. You might want to bring a pole and cast for large-mouth bass, bluegill, or go deep for channel cats.

Here at Hontoon Island, you will see plenty of nature and your worries will seem a million miles away. So bring plenty of food and gear. You might be here a long time.

To get there from FL 44 in Deland, turn left on Old New York Avenue and follow it for 2.5 miles. Turn left on Hontoon Road and follow it for 2 miles. Turn left on River Ridge Road and follow it for 0.5 mile to the ferry landing.

KEY INFORMATION

Hontoon Island Campground
2309 River Ridge Road
Deland, FL 32720

Operated by: Florida State Parks

Information: (904) 736-5309

Open: Year-round

Individual sites: 12

Each site has: Picnic table, fire ring

Site assignment: Assigned by ranger unless specific sight asked for

Registration: At Park Headquar-ters; all campsites can be reserved

Facilities: Hot showers, flush toilets, water spigots, camp store

Parking: At ferry landing only

Fee: $9 per night

Elevation: 25 feet

Restrictions

Pets—Prohibited

Fires—In fire rings only

Alcoholic beverages—Prohibited

Vehicles—Not allowed on island

Other—14-day stay limit

JUNIPER SPRINGS CAMPGROUND

Ocala

This recreation area was well developed in the 1930s and is well taken care of today. Clear, 72° F Juniper Springs is the centerpiece of this Ocala National Forest landmark. The springs well up at 13 million gallons per day into continental America's only subtropical national forest. The campground is aesthetically integrated into the landscape and has a separate loop for tent campers only.

The campground is divided into three loops. The first loop is the 34-site Tropic Camp Area. Palm trees, live oak, and southern hardwoods shade the campsites, which have adequate privacy thanks to the understory of palmetto. The 17 campsites on the outside of the paved loop are pull-through sites designed for RVs. The pull-in sites on the inside of the loop have less room but are closer to one of the two modern comfort stations. Warm showers are available in one of the comfort stations. Though this loop is attractive, the presence of RVs makes it the least-appealing loop.

The Sandpine Camp Area has 25 drive-up campsites on a paved loop. A primarily pine canopy makes for a brighter, more open campsite. Thick vegetation buffers yield the maximum in site privacy. The eight campsites on the inside of the loop are closer to the centrally located comfort station and its flush toilets for each sex. However, there is no shower. This is the second-most-desirable and least-used loop.

CAMPGROUND RATINGS

Beauty:	★★★★★
Site privacy:	★★★
Site spaciousness:	★★★
Quiet:	★★★
Security:	★★★★★
Cleanliness/upkeep:	★★★★

Millions of gallons of water, thousands of acres of wilderness, and 19 tent-only campsites add up to make Juniper Springs a winning number.

The best loop is the Fern Hammock Tent Camp Area. The paved road ends and the campsites begin beneath a tall canopy of palm trees and southern hardwoods such as hickory. Three campsites on the main road are immediately followed by a spur loop with six sites near a low-lying area.

Three campsites are on a small dead end beside Fern Hammock Springs. The other four campsites are near the loop comfort station, which has warm showers. This loop has the thinnest understory, mostly ground cover; however, this will give you a chance to meet your fellow tent campers.

Water spigots are well placed throughout this attractive, well-kept campground. The whole recreation area has received a makeover recently. Overall, the campsites are spacious, clean, and camper-friendly.

Summer weekends are the busy time here; the campground will fill. But other than that, you should have no problem getting a campsite. Winter is a good time to visit; mosquitoes are less of a problem. The springs stay at 72° F year-round, and the warm days and cool nights make for ideal camping conditions.

Juniper Springs attracts swimmers no matter what the season. The area where the water bubbles up was lined with concrete and rock by the Civilian Conservation Corps. It serves as a natural swimming pool. Concrete steps lead into the waters, where snorkelers kick around amid sunbathers cooling off from the Florida sun.

Trails lead through all of the camping loops to both Fern Hammock Spring and Juniper Spring. A three-quarter-mile-long, self-interpretive nature trail starts at Juniper Springs and follows Juniper Creek. Learn about this ecosystem that thrives where north meets south.

The most popular activity here at Juniper Springs is canoeing. A 7-mile one-way trip leads from the springs to Juniper Wayside Park near Lake George. Float the translucent waters on the narrow creek through the heart of the 13,000-acre Juniper Prairie Wilderness. Cypress trees line the waterway, along with palms and other hardwoods. Motorboat enthusiasts have nearby Lake George, Florida's second-largest lake, to enjoy all manner of activities.

Long- or short-distance hikers can enjoy a portion of the Florida National Scenic Trail. It heads in either direction near the campground entrance booth. The northerly portion of the trail enters the Juniper Prairie Wilderness, passing many small lakes and Juniper Creek itself before leaving the wilderness after 9 miles.

Come and enjoy this natural, well-cared-for showpiece of the Ocala National Forest.

To get there from Ocala, drive east on State Hwy. 40 for 28 miles. Juniper Springs Recreation Area will be on your left.

KEY INFORMATION

Juniper Springs Campground
26701 East State Road
Silver Springs, FL 34488

Operated by: U.S. Forest Service

Information: (352) 625-3147

Open: Year-round

Individual sites: 79

Each site has: Tent pad, concrete picnic table, fire ring

Site assignment: First come, first served; no reservations

Registration: At campground entrance booth

Facilities: Hot showers, flush toilets, water spigots, pay phone, camp store

Parking: At campsites only

Fee: $10.75 per night tent loop, $12.75 per night other loops

Elevation: 45 feet

Restrictions

  Pets—On leash only

  Fires—In fire rings only

  Alcoholic beverages—At campsites only

  Vehicles—None

  Other—14-day stay limit

LAKE EATON CAMPGROUND

Ocala

Lake Eaton has undergone renovation in recent years. That is not to say it has been developed. On the contrary, the campground was reduced and organized. The appealing natural setting was already there, in the heart of the Ocala National Forest. Lake Eaton itself and other nearby locales in the forest afford visitors many recreational opportunities.

The campground is located on the shores of Lake Eaton, amidst a forest of tall pines and live oak, which spread their shade-giving branches throughout the area. A few palms grace the forest, giving it that semitropical look. A thick ground cover of brushy oaks and a smattering of palmettos lend an in-the-forest feel to Lake Eaton Campground.

The camping area is organized in the classic loop fashion, stretched out along a packed dirt road. The first three campsites are single sites on the outside of the loop. Campsite 1, at the beginning of the loop, is somewhat open, but after that the woods take over. These sites are very spacious, but the double sites, 4 through 6, are really large. They are set back farther on the loop and have two concrete picnic tables each. The pine needles and oak leaves get really thick back here.

The next five campsites are on the outside of the loop as it doubles back around. These sites are the most private. However, nearly all the campsites at Lake Eaton fea-

CAMPGROUND RATINGS

Beauty:	★★★★
Site privacy:	★★★★
Site spaciousness:	★★★★★
Quiet:	★★★★★
Security:	★★★
Cleanliness/upkeep:	★★★

Lake Eaton offers a quiet and remote camping experience in the Ocala National Forest.

ture superlative privacy and spaciousness. These five sites are closest to the lake and have a somewhat obscured view of Lake Eaton. The final two campsites are large single sites and are the only two on the inside of the campground loop.

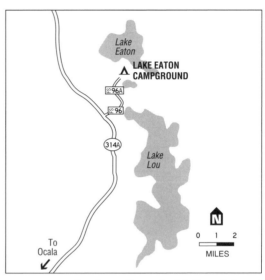

A pit toilet for each sex lies in the center of the loop. The old-fashioned hand-pump water well is near campsite 12. These rustic facilities encourage hardier tent campers, though a few RV-driving "snowbirds" can be seen here during the winter. Tent campers are the norm year-round. Don't imagine some rough place, though. National forest campgrounds are generally less developed.

This locale of natural beauty just needed a little organization. The Forest Service has built a boat ramp, but this body of water spells canoe for me. A fishing and observation pier has been erected near the campground. Lake Eaton has fine fishing, and the pier is a good place to watch the clouds roll by. Relaxation comes naturally here.

But don't get lazy. There are a pair of trails nearby that would be a shame to miss, being so informative and so close. Head back out to Forest Road 96 and take a left. Drive about half a mile, then take another left on FS 79. Soon you'll come to the Eaton Sinkhole Trail and the Lake Eaton Loop Trail.

The Sinkhole Trail was the highlight of my day. It forms a 2-mile loop and passes through a sand scrub forest to a place where the limestone strata, 120 feet below the surface, has eroded. The land above it collapsed and formed the sinkhole. The sinkhole is like an inverted island of moist flora surrounded by the drier sand scrub forest. Plaques and displays explain this process. Do not miss this trail.

The 2.1-mile Lake Eaton Loop Trail starts across the road and descends from the dry, hilly woods to the cypress that borders Lake Eaton. Side paths lead to observation points on the lake. When I was there, I tagged along on a guided hike for bird-watchers.

Many other nearby natural lakes grace the immediate area. Lake Lou and Fore Lake are two that have forest access. The Ocklawaha River is minutes away and offers a canoeing experience of its own. A map of the Ocala National Forest will help you navigate your way through the 430,000 acres it encompasses. No matter what you do in the Ocala National Forest, Lake Eaton will be a fine place to return, as others do, year after year.

To get there from Ocala, drive east on FL 40 for about 17 miles. Turn left on CR 314A, follow it for about 5 miles, then turn right on FS 96. Follow FS 96 for .5 mile. Turn left on FS 96A and drive 1 mile. Lake Eaton Campground will be on your right.

KEY INFORMATION

Lake Eaton Campground
17147 East State Highway 40
Silver Springs, FL 34488

Operated by: U.S. Forest Service

Information: (352) 625-2520

Open: Year-round

Individual sites: 13

Each site has: Picnic table, fire ring, lantern post

Site assignment: First come, first served; no reservations

Registration: Self-registration on site

Facilities: Pit toilet, hand-pumped water

Parking: At campsites only

Fee: $3 per night single site, $5 per night double site

Elevation: 40 feet

Restrictions

Pets—On 6-foot leash only

Fires—In fire rings only

Alcoholic beverages—At camp-sites only

Vehicles—None

Other—14-day stay limit

LAKE KISSIMMEE CAMPGROUND

Lake Wales

L ake Kissimmee State Park lies in a remote section of the citrus, lake, and cattle country of central Florida. The park lies on the shores of the state's third-largest lake, a lake renowned for its angling opportunities. The shady campground is ideal for tent campers who want to see a lot of water, some of real Florida's woods, and a living history demonstration of the Florida cowboy of the 1800s.

Lake Kissimmee Campground is divided into two loops, with a major distinction between the two loops. Loop A has 30 campsites situated in a forest of live oak and pine. Clumps of palmetto shield campers from one another. The sites have plenty of room, especially toward the end of the loop. Twelve of the sites are on the inside of the loop along with the comfort station, featuring hot showers and flush toilets. Four short trails lead from the loop road to the comfort station.

The major characteristic that distinguishes Loop A from Loop B is the water and electricity available at each campsite on Loop A. In the winter, this can spell RV-driving "snowbirds," though Lake Kissimmee is at the northern end of the snowbird belt. So, your best bet is Loop B.

Loop B also has 30 campsites, 13 of which are inside the loop. This campground is a little more piney but has its share of live oaks, providing shade and scenic value to your campsite. Four paths

CAMPGROUND RATINGS

Beauty: ★★★★
Site privacy: ★★★
Site spaciousness: ★★★
Quiet: ★★★★
Security: ★★★★★
Cleanliness/upkeep: ★★★★

Living history and a quality campground are set on the shores of scenic Lake Kissimmee.

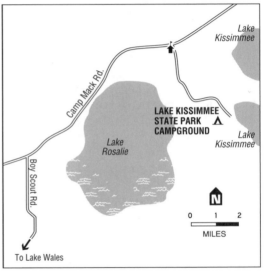

lead from the loop road to the centrally located bathhouse with hot showers and flush toilets. There is no electricity on this loop. Water spigots are located at the beginning of each footpath that leads to the comfort station.

On my weekday visit to Lake Kissimmee, I had Loop B all to myself. Loop A had some snowbirds and a few tenters. This underused state park is busy only during winter weekends and holidays. The rest of the time you can nearly have the run of the place. But weekday visitors miss out on the living history demonstration of the Florida cowboy at an actual location of a ranch back in 1876.

Here you'll find a frontier cowboy who will be going about the daily routine of his life. You can visit with him and ask questions about what his life is like. But he knows nothing about events after 1876. His whip is his tool for controlling his scrub cattle. His cracking of his whip came to be his signature, hence the nickname for these Florida cowboys as "crackers."

These crackers tended scrub cows—small, lean bovine descended from cattle brought by Spanish explorers. This life of the Florida cowboy is overshadowed by the cowboys of the West and makes Kissimmee State Park not only a natural preserve but a historic one as well.

On the natural side, there are 13 miles of nature trails that comb the nine plant communities of this park, ranging from prairies to pine flatwoods. Two major trails each form a loop for a good day hike. The 6-mile North Loop Trail winds around the Park Drive. The park's best trail spurs off of this one, the Gobbler Ridge Trail. It travels 1 mile over Gobbler Ridge, overlooking the huge Lake Kissimmee. Start getting your views after you top the ridge.

The other major trail is the 6.7-mile Buster Island Trail. It traverses the more remote south end of the park. Here you stand a better chance of seeing deer, bobcats, turkeys, and other wildlife. If you are rushed for time, at least climb the observation tower. It is a short walk to the observation tower located near the picnic area. The wooden tower rises over the live oaks and looks out on the grassy plain and the waters of Lake Kissimmee.

The park has its very own boat launch for anglers. You can fish for largemouth bass, bream, and other warm-water fish. Swimming is not permitted, though. As the park brochure states, boredom is strictly prohibited. But if you want to relax beneath the live oaks, that's not a bad idea either.

To get there from Lake Wales, drive east on FL 60 for 12 miles. Turn left on Boy Scout Road and follow it for 3 miles. Turn right on Camp Mack Road and follow it for 5 miles. Lake Kissimmee State Park will be on your right.

KEY INFORMATION

Lake Kissimmee
14248 Camp Mack Road
Lake Wales, FL 33853

Operated by: Florida State Parks

Information: (941) 696-1112

Open: Year-round

Individual sites: 60

Each site has: 30 have picnic table and fire ring; 30 have picnic table, fire ring, water, and electricity

Site assignment: Assigned by ranger unless specific site asked for

Registration: By phone or at park entrance booth

Facilities: Hot showers, flush toilets, water spigots

Parking: At campsites and extra car parking

Fee: $8 per night April to October, $12 per night November to March; $2 electrcity fee

Elevation: 65 feet

Restrictions

Pets—On leash only

Fires—In fire grates only

Alcoholic beverages—Prohibited

Vehicles—None

Other—14-day stay limit

LITTLE MANATEE RIVER CAMPGROUND

Sun City Center

Little Manatee River State Recreation Area has been a recent acquisition in the Florida State Park system. A good network of hiking and horseback-riding trails has been constructed and the Little Manatee River is one of Florida's best canoeing experiences. The campground was supposed to be three times its present size, but lucky for us the state ran out of funding. Now, the campground is just the right size and is tastefully integrated into the natural environment.

The recreation area is one of Florida's lesser-known jewels. The campground shines brightly. At the rear of the park, enter the campground on a packed-gravel road. Much of the mature vegetation of the campground area was left intact—sabal palm, sand pine, and scrub oaks. Many trees are covered in Spanish moss. A very thick understory of brush shields campers from one another.

Little Manatee River uses a circular-loop design to disperse the campsites. Most campsites have ample room for any gear-toting tent camper. Eleven of the campsites are on the inside of the loop. The campsites toward the end of the loop are more open and grassy with a lot of palm tees, but that is only relative to the rest of the dense campground. This gives you an option if you don't like heavily wooded sites.

In the center of the loop is a comfort station with hot showers, flush toilets, and a laundry

CAMPGROUND RATINGS

Beauty: ★★★
Site privacy: ★★★★
Site spaciousness: ★★★
Quiet: ★★★★
Security: ★★★★★
Cleanliness/upkeep: ★★★★

One of Florida's newer state recreation areas has one of its better campgrounds.

area. Little Manatee River can be busy with "snowbirds" anytime between December and March. But even then, the sites offer such good campsite privacy that you won't be bothered by a few RVs. The rest of the year is slow. In the summer, you can "shoot off a shotgun in four directions and not hit anybody," according to one ranger. Summer weekends may see a few visitors.

Good trails have been constructed here. Developed by the Florida Trails Association, the Little Manatee River Hiking Trail starts in the parking area off U.S. 301. It follows Little Manatee River downstream for 1.6 miles before crossing Cypress Creek. The trail then follows the river awhile longer before turning away and heading upstream away from the river. Then it returns to U.S. 301. All day hikers must register at the park office before they use this trail. Down from the picnic area is the Oxbow Nature Trail. It circles an oxbow lake that was once part of the Little Manatee River. I walked this sandy trail on a sunny day; seeing the river made me want to canoe it. So I did.

The Canoe Outpost on the Little Manatee River offers shuttled trips at reasonable rates. I chose the 6.5-mile trip that starts on U.S. 301 and ends at the park. The river, at its winter-low levels, had many overhangs leaning from its steep forest banks. It certainly lived up to its status as an Outstanding Florida Water. Below the park, the river widens and becomes influenced by the tides. The river offers both fresh and saltwater fishing depending on where you are. The telephone number for the Canoe Outpost is (813) 634-2228.

There are also 12 miles of horse trails meandering through the park. The Dude Lake Horse Trail and the Mustang Horse Trail both form loops and traverse the pine scrub terrain. There are no horses for rent, but hikers can walk these trails. Watch where you step.

I like the slow pace and relaxed feel of this park. The campground is scenic and melds into its natural surroundings. The Little Manatee River is one of my favorite Florida waterways. Come venture to the park that the rushed Florida vacationers pass by.

To get there from Sun City Center, drive south on U.S. 301 for 5 miles. Turn right on Lightfoot Road. Little Manatee River State Park will be on right after a short distance.

KEY INFORMATION

Little Manatee River Campground
215 Lightfoot Road
Wimauma, FL 33598

Operated by: Florida State Parks

Information: (813) 671-5005

Open: Year-round

Individual sites: 30

Each site has: Picnic table, fire ring, water, electricity

Site assignment: Assigned by ranger unless specific site asked for

Registration: By phone or at park entrance booth

Facilities: Hot shower, flush toilets, pay phone, laundry

Parking: At campsites only

Fee: $10 per night; $2 electricity fee

Elevation: 5 feet

Restrictions

Pets—Prohibited

Fires—In fire rings only

Alcoholic beverages—Prohibited

Vehicles—None

CENTRAL FLORIDA

MUTUAL MINE CAMPGROUND

Inverness

This is a different campground. First, it is one of two that I've seen that are only open on weekends. Plus, it is located around an abandoned phosphate mine. Don't worry; it's safe around here. The lake filled in after the hand-dug mine was abandoned in 1914. But time, nature, and the Florida Division of Forestry have teamed up to make this a picturesque little campground. The forestry people have also constructed many miles of hiking trails nearby, and Mutual Mine is now for fish only. Florida's most unusual state park, Homosassa Springs State Wildlife Park, is just a short drive away.

The Mutual Mine Campground entrance road splits into two spur roads. One road has six campsites, and the other seven. They are divided by the lake that was once Mutual Mine. The level ground above the mine is covered by a mixed forest of live oak and pine trees. The campground has a grassy understory that seems like a lawn. The grass is broken up by stained wooden poles that divide campsites from one another.

The spur road to the right enters an open forest of mature pines. It seems as if the area has been landscaped. The first two campsites are in this pine wood, which is carpeted by needles over the grass. The campsites are open and spacious. The next two campsites are shaded by live oaks and a stray turkey oak.

CAMPGROUND RATINGS

Beauty: ★★★★★
Site privacy: ★★★
Site spaciousness: ★★★★★
Quiet: ★★
Security: ★★★
Cleanliness/upkeep: ★★★★

It may sound odd to camp by an abandoned mine, but this is one of Florida's prettiest campgrounds.

There is a great distance between all the campsites, which makes up for the lack of understory. The spur road ends in a loop and holds the final two sites, which are in a thicket of laurel and live oak. These sites are spacious as well and have an obscured view of the lake.

The spur road to the left also begins in an open pine forest. The first campsite is obscured by young trees, but the next four are in the pines and have immense "yards" on which to stake a tent. Live oaks begin at the fourth site. Wooden poles divide the sites on this loop road as well.

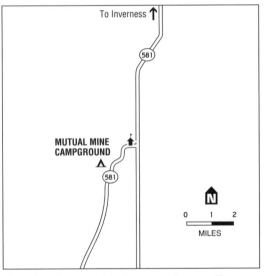

The road bends around the lake and contains two very private sites. The woods are dense and the shade is heavy. The sites are separated from each other and the rest of the campground by trees and distance. Farther along, the spur road turns around.

This attractive campground feels small already, but the two spur roads make it look like two distinct campgrounds. The two roads share a common bathroom area, located at the beginning of the right-hand road. There are two shedlike structures that house clean flush toilets for each sex. Water spigots are spread throughout the campground.

You can get a closer look into the old mine via the nature trail that winds along the lake's shoreline. It starts at the wooden stairway leading down to it. The half-hour walk goes up and down along the steep banks of the lake. Numbered signs accompany a handout that explains the nature of the area. Though the lake may be partly covered in algae, a ranger told me the fishing was good here. The lake can be accessed at several points along the rugged little trail.

Also at the campground is a trailhead for the 46 miles of trails in the Citrus Tract of the Withalacoochee State Forest. A board at the trailhead shows you the loop possibilities. The Citrus Hiking Trail is blazed in orange. You can stay dry-footed (providing it doesn't rain, which happened during my trip here) and pass through several forest communities, including sandhill scrub, stands of turkey oak, and live oak thickets. The hiking combinations are limited only by your stamina, though Mansfield Pond is a good destination.

At Homosassa Springs Wildlife Park you can see all sorts of wild animals, including bears, bobcats, and birds. Boat tours are available of the Springs of 10,000 Fish. You will probably see a manatee. Since the park is state run, you know this is not some fly-by-night sideshow. Check it out. It is west of Inverness on U.S. 19.

Mutual Mine is an off-the-beaten-path campground where RVs are as rare as the bad experiences. Pick your site in the pines or beneath the live oaks. Just remember to make sure it is on a Friday, Saturday, or Sunday night if you go during the months of January through July.

To get there from U.S. 41 in Inverness, drive west for 0.5 mile on FL 44. Turn left on CR 581 and follow it for 5 miles. Mutual Mine will be on your right.

KEY INFORMATION

Mutual Mine Campground
15019 Broad Street
Brooksville, FL 34601

Operated by: Florida Division of Forestry

Information: (904) 754-6777

Open: Daily August to December; Friday, Saturday, and Sunday January to July

Individual sites: 13

Each site has: Picnic table, fire grate

Site assignment: First come, first served; no reservations

Registration: Ranger will come by and register you

Facilities: Flush toilets, water spigots

Parking: At campsites only

Fee: $12 per night

Elevation: 50 feet

Restrictions

Pets—Prohibited

Fires—In fire grates only

Alcoholic beverages—Prohibited

Vehicles—None

Other—14-day stay limit

SALT SPRINGS CAMPGROUND
Ocala

Don't be alarmed when you first pull into Salt Springs Campground—it looks like RV hell. This is *not* where you camp. There is a separate area for primitive campers, which in this case means tent campers. The primitive campground shows some signs of wear but will make do when you realize the recreational potential of Salt Springs.

The Forest Service eventually plans to remodel the campground—when it gets the money. But for now, the primitive area will pass muster. It starts at the back of the RV area, closer to Salt Springs. The whole campground is on a slight slope that ends at the Salt Springs Run.

Overhead is a thick canopy of live oak trees that shade almost the entire primitive area. The understory is decidedly lacking, though the thick tree trunks do break up the campground. Fallen oak leaves and sand form the campground floor. The first 18 campsites are laid out in a one-way-in, one-way-out series of small packed-sand roads. These are the least spacious and desirable campsites in the primitive area, though they are passable.

The next group of campsites are laid out on a spur road that eventually turns into the footpath to the springs. These sites are large and open. Being close to the springs can be good or bad, depending on how you look at it—good because the springs are close, bad because other campers walk by on their way to the springs.

CAMPGROUND RATINGS

Beauty: ★★★
Site privacy: ★★
Site spaciousness: ★★★★
Quiet: ★★
Security: ★★★★
Cleanliness/upkeep: ★★★

Salt Springs is a bit on the developed side, but that sometimes happens with particularly scenic areas as this one.

The campground road loops back around to the most open section of the primitive area. Here grassy plots and live oaks share space on the inside of the loop. The campground boat launch spurs off this area. Several sites on the outside of the loop are located well back from the road and offer the most privacy in the campground. These are the most desirable campsites.

Two bathhouses serve the primitive area. Both have hot showers and flush toilets. One is at the primitive area entrance and the other is at the back of the campground—not too far to walk for anyone. Water spigots are conveniently placed throughout the campground.

The primitive area at Salt Springs is busy during the summer, especially on weekends. I came here during late January and had the whole campground to myself. I walked the footpath to the springs. Here, seven different vents surge forth water. The water is mineral rich and has a slightly salty taste. Don't be misled; it's not like the ocean. As a matter of fact, the spring is teeming with freshwater fish.

Salt Springs is also teeming with swimmers during the warmer months. The varied aquatic life and differing water depths lure snorkelers into the 72° F water, too. Others try to see the fish at the end of their line. Largemouth bass, bluegill, and catfish can be caught from here to Lake George.

A few water lovers use motorboats—it's only 4 miles down the spring run to Lake George. Others prefer to canoe. A quiet canoe will enhance your chances for seeing some of the thriving bird life along Salt Springs Run. Herons, osprey, hawks, and even bald eagles are often sighted.

The Salt Springs Trail is another way to see wildlife here. It starts back on State Road 19, a short distance from the campground. You'll pass through many of central Florida's forest communities to end at an observation platform at the spring run. Maybe you'll see an alligator or two. Other nearby attractions are Silver Glen Springs, where the water looks sky-blue. Hikers can walk from the campground on a 4.6-mile connector trail that leads to the Florida National Scenic Trail.

Water is an ever-present natural feature in the state of Florida. These springs are nature's way of allowing us one more opportunity to get our feet wet. Camp in the primitive area beneath the live oaks of Salt Springs and take your shoes off.

To get there from Ocala, drive east on FL 40 for 12 miles, then turn left on CR 314 for 18 miles. Turn left on State Hwy. 19 and follow it for 0.5 mile to Salt Springs Campground, which will be on your right.

**Salt Springs Campground
17147 East State Highway 40
Silver Springs, FL 34488**

Operated by: U.S. Forest Service

Information: (352) 685-2048

Open: Year-round

Individual sites: 57 primitive

Each site has: Picnic table, fire grate, lantern post

Site assignment: First come, first served; no reservations

Registration: At campground office

Facilities: Hot showers, flush toilets, water spigots, pay phone

Parking: At campsites only

Fee: $10 per night

Elevation: 45 feet

Restrictions

Pets—On 6-foot leash only

Fires—In fire grates only

Alcoholic beverages—Prohibited

Vehicles—None

TOMOKA CAMPGROUND

Ormond Beach

Enter Tomoka State Park from Ormond Beach. Instantly, a dense forest envelops the road. But this forest is just one element of Tomoka; water, salt marsh, and history meld together to create a coastal slice of the real Florida. The junglesque campground is a delight for campers. The nonelectric sites separate tent campers from the RV campers.

The campground is arranged in a rectangular loop divided by three short crossroads. The vast majority of the campsites are located on the outside of the loop. Electric campsites cover the first two-thirds of the campground. The back of the campground is nonelectric and that is where tent campers will desire to stay.

The campground backs up to a small inlet of the Halifax River, a saltwater waterway between the mainland and barrier islands. The lush forest is dominated by live oaks, draped in Spanish moss and resurrection ferns. The overhead canopy lets in slivers of sunlight. Palmetto, hardwood seedlings, and dense brush grow everywhere around and between the campsites.

Campsites 1 through 35 are electric. Then the string of 36 primitive sites starts and circles around the back of the campground loop. All but five of the sites are on the outside of the loop. Campsite privacy is at a maximum here. Vegetation creeps up on every campsite, actually sacrificing some

CAMPGROUND RATINGS

Beauty:	★★★★★
Site privacy:	★★★★
Site spaciousness:	★★
Quiet:	★★★
Security:	★★★★
Cleanliness/upkeep:	★★★★★

Tomoka has one of Florida's most attractive oceanside campgrounds.

on campsite spaciousness. It seems like another world out here.

Electric campsites resume as the loop returns to its beginning. Three comfort stations serve the campground. They are spaced throughout the campground to reach all campers. All have hot showers and flush toilets, but only the first two have a pay phone.

Winter will find a few "snowbird" campers, but they are concentrated in the electric section. Spring and early summer are the busiest times here.

The nonelectric sites are almost always available, except during Bike Week in nearby Daytona Beach.

The woods weren't always so thick here. In the late 1700s, a man named Richard Oswald cleared some of the forest to plant indigo, a plant used for dye. He was preceded by the Timucuan Indians, who actually had a village here. They lived off the rich estuaries that surround the park peninsula. The forest has obviously recovered well and holds its own against many of the old-growth trees that dot Tomoka.

Today, the estuaries are still rich. The Tomoka and Halifax Rivers hold snook, flounder, redfish, and sea trout. Bait your line with live shrimp and throw it in. The small creeks and grassy marshes are fun to paddle. Tomoka has a boat launch and canoes are available for rent. Keep the tides in mind when you plan your canoe trip.

You can walk the small beach on the north end of the park or walk the nature trail to the park museum, which explains life in this area, both past and present. Tomoka also has a small unit at its south end with two fishing and observation piers overlooking the coastal marsh.

You can't complete your visit without going to nearby Bulow Creek State Park. It is centered around a special 800-year-old oak tree, the Fairchild oak. The tree sits on the site of an old plantation. Step back in time on the nature trail there. Also nearby is the Bulow Plantation Ruins State Historic Site. See the remains of a bygone way of life and learn the history of the plantation. Get directions to these places from the park office. To reach a beach directly on the Atlantic, drive back to State Road 40 and turn left. You will drive right to Ormond Beach.

If you like a thick, woodsy campground on the edge of the ocean, you will like Tomoka. It makes a good base camp for all the nearby attractions, including Daytona Beach. This campground ranks right up there with the most picturesque in the state.

To get there from SR 40 in Ormond Beach, turn left on Beach Street. Follow it for 3 miles to Tomoka State Park.

KEY INFORMATION

Tomoka Campground
2099 North Beach Street
Ormond Beach, FL 32174

Operated by: Florida State Parks

Information: (904) 676-4050

Open: Year-round

Individual sites: 62 electric, 33 nonelectric

Each site has: Picnic table, fire grate, water spigot

Site assignment: Assigned by ranger unless specific site asked for

Registration: By phone or at park entrance booth

Facilities: Hot showers, flush toilets, pay phone

Parking: At campsites and extra car parking

Fee: $8 per night June to January, $15 per night February to May; $2 electricity fee

Elevation: Sea Level

Restrictions

Pets—Prohibited

Fires—In fire grates only

Alcoholic beverages—Prohibited

Vehicles—None

Other—14-day stay limit

SOUTH
FLORIDA

BAHIA HONDA CAMPGROUND
Marathon

B ahia Honda is Florida's southernmost state park, hence the southernmost state park in the United States. And the ecosystem here is as unique as its geographical distinction. Two of the three separate campgrounds here are ideal for tent campers. And the other one, well, that's for the RV gang.

Being so far south and so close to Key West makes Bahia Honda busy, especially in winter. Make your reservations 60 days in advance, even though half the sites are first come, first served. Campers tend to plant themselves once they get a site at Bahia Honda. If you must take a site in the RV area, take it, then get on the waiting list to transfer to another site.

The Buttonwood Camping Area is the one for RVs. It is the most open and the closest to U.S. 1. If you have a boat, it has a campside marina just for campers. Buttonwood also has a full bathhouse. Fifteen sites are oceanside, but it seems more like a parking lot by the sea.

The Sandspur Camping Area is closest to Sandspur Beach, consistently rated as one of the best beaches in America. The camping area is not too bad, either. It contains 24 campsites arranged in linear fashion along a spur road. The first eight sites are cut into the beachside woodland. The beach is across the spur road. These sites are well shaded but could be hot and buggy on windless days.

CAMPGROUND RATINGS

Beauty:	★★★★
Site privacy:	★★★
Site spaciousness:	★★★
Quiet:	★★
Security:	★★★
Cleanliness/upkeep:	★★★

Bahia Honda has the finest beach in the Keys, and a whole lot more.

Past the bathhouse, camp-
sites are situated on both sides
of the road. Five more sites are
nestled in the woods. The
other side of the road contains
11 beachside campsites that
are the most desirable at Bahia
Honda. These campsites, as all
in the Sandspur area, have
well-grown campsite buffers.

The Bay Side Camping Area
is the smallest and most isolated. You must pass through the
Buttonwood Camping Area and
drive under the low clearance of
U.S. 1, which effectively cuts off
all but standard passenger cars.
Pass a bathhouse with no showers and come to the eight wooded sites. These
sites, across the road from the Gulf, curve around a small bay.

I recommend the Sandspur Camping Area over the others. It is most suitable for tent campers and is closest to the best beach at Bahia Honda,
Sandspur Beach. There are two other beaches here, Calusa Beach and Logger
Head Beach. Calusa Beach is in the Gulf, but looks out on busy U.S. 1 and is
adjacent to the main marina. Logger Head Beach is on the Atlantic and has
nothing but a view of those colorful Key waters.

These beaches can get mighty hot any time of year. But each one has
swimmer-friendly waters, the best swimming in the Keys. The water is never
too cold, even in winter. Fishermen enjoy these waters as well. Tarpon, when
in season, is the most desired species. Launch your boat at the marina or hire
a guide.

One unusual aspect of Bahia Honda is the old bridge. It is the now-closed
span that used to connect Bahia Honda Key with West Summerland Key. A
trail to the old bridge leaves near Logger Head Beach. Follow the span as it
rises over the waters below. It's probably as high as you will get in the Keys.

Another walk is the nature trail that enters the real Florida at the north end of the Sandspur Beach.

No trip this far south is complete without a trip to Key West. Ernest Hemingway's town is a tourist attraction, yet it is steeped in history. The narrow roads can be congested, but relax and join in the parade. Check out Duval Street, a mecca for tourists; Old Town, with its elegant homes; and Mallory Square, with its street entertainers.

The best way to do this may seem corny at first, but swallow your pride, don your shades, and ride the Conch Tour Train. It's the ultimate in tourist schlock, but you will learn much about the history of this southernmost city in the United States. Then you can drive back to your campsite at Bahia Honda with a complete taste of the Keys.

To get there from Marathon, drive 12 miles south to Bahia Honda Recreation Area. Turn left into the state park entrance.

KEY INFORMATION

Bahia Honda Campground
36850 Overseas Highway
Big Pine Key, FL 33043

Operated by: Florida State Parks

Information: (305) 872-2353

Open: Year-round

Individual sites: 60 electric, 20 nonelectric

Each site has: Picnic table, fire grill, water

Site assignment: Assigned by ranger unless specific site asked for

Registration: By phone or at park entrance booth

Facilities: Hot showers, flush toilets, pay phones

Parking: At campsites only

Fee: $24 per night; $2 electricity fee

Elevation: Sea level

Restrictions

Pets—Prohibited

Fires—In fire grills only

Alcoholic beverages—Prohibited

Vehicles—None

Other—14-day stay limit

BEAR ISLAND CAMPGROUND

Everglades City

This is the most remote and rustic campground you will find in this guidebook. But that is only fitting, for the Big Cypress National Preserve is a remote and rugged place. Vast tracts of cypress trees, pine woods, hardwood forests, and grassy prairies intermingle in reaction to the timeless battle between water and land. Your adventure in the Big Cypress is limited only to how daring you are. A system of marked trails emanates from Bear Island Campground, offering a glimpse into a strange and beautiful ecosystem.

The campground begins shortly after the final right turn from Turner River Road. The vault toilets for the campground are located at the turn. After you pass the first old cattle guard, a road turns left. This road leads to an open field, bordered on one side by woodland and on the other side by freshwater prairie. The field offers views across the grass to thick hammocks—islands of trees. The woods here are so exotic. They are heavy on the palm trees, with Dade County pine and a few live oaks.

The main campground continues on the primary road. Here you will see marked sites that pull off on either side of the road. There is ample space between most sites. Large grassy areas usually have a fire ring in them. Thick stands of palmetto offer all the privacy a camper will want.

Some sites are far back from the road and are ringed in palms with pines over them.

CAMPGROUND RATINGS

Beauty:	★★★★
Site privacy:	★★★★
Site spaciousness:	★★★★★
Quiet:	★★★★
Security:	★★
Cleanliness/upkeep:	★★

Bear Island is the best tent campers' campground in the Big Cypress National Preserve. Be warned: This campground is ultrarustic, very remote, and very beautiful.

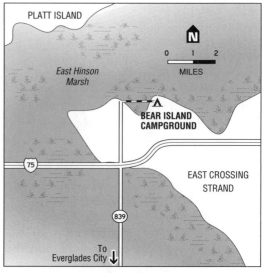

Other sites back against an open prairie that look out on stands of cypress in the distance. As you press on, another cattle guard crosses the road. This is the end of the campground and the beginning of a trail. By the way, get a trail map of the Bear Island area at the Oasis Visitor Center or at the Wildlife Check-in Station near the campground.

Bear Island is often used by hunters and off-road vehicle enthusiasts. Don't worry, though, these folks love the wilderness as much as you do. If you can, hook up with one of them and watch each other's stuff. This place is very remote, but its remoteness is two-sided. Because most people won't casually venture here, your privacy is virtually guaranteed. The downside, however, is that help, should you require it, could be a long time in coming. As for me, I wouldn't worry about it beyond taking normal precautions. I firmly believe you are safer in nearly any wilderness setting than in nearly any urban setting.

By the way, don't come here during the summer unless you have a good tent, bug spray, and a hearty constitution. The bugs here can be very wicked. My trip took place during February. I watched the sun sink over the palms and made a small fire. The hamburgers were delicious and the stars overhead were a sight to behold. I bedded down early, then arose at first light. The land was shrouded in fog. I walked east and made a loop. Palms, marsh, and pines faded in and out of view. Hordes of birds noisily sang from the grassy marsh, unseen but well heard.

Later, the day warmed, and I took an auto tour of the preserve. Alligators and birds commanded the roadside canals. I bounced along the scenic Loop

Road. Sunlight intermittently pierced the swamp, where water so clear amazed me as much as the variety of bird life did. Fishermen lazily hung on to cane poles wherever there was open water.

I walked a portion of the Florida National Scenic Trail. Here, in the preserve, the Florida Trail starts its ultimate journey to northwest Florida. It begins right behind the Oasis Visitor Center on U.S. 41.

Some people ride airboats in the preserve. Others drive big swamp buggies—you've got to see one to believe it. The Miccosukee Indians, who inhabit portions of the preserve, offer tourist rides for a fee in both of these vehicles. It may sound hokey, but it is really a fun way to see a part of this place.

Bear Island is your best bet for camping in the preserve. Make sure to bring all the water you will need. The camping is free and very rustic. This upper half of the Everglades ecosystem is what makes south Florida very different from what most people think about the area. Camp at Bear Island and get to the bare essence of what tent camping is all about.

To get there from Everglades City, drive east on U.S. 41 for 10 miles. Turn left on CR 839 (Turner River Road) and follow it for 19 miles, passing under I-75. Continue 1.3 miles beyond I-75 and turn right. Follow the gravel road for 1.5 miles, passing the Wildlife Check-in Station on the way. The road will run into Bear Island Campground.

KEY INFORMATION

Bear Island Campground
Star Route Box 110
Ochopee, FL 33943

Operated by: Big Cypress National Preserve

Information: (813) 695-2000

Open: Year-round

Individual sites: 20

Each site has: Fire ring

Site assignment: First come, first served; no reservation

Registration: None

Facilities: Vault toilet

Parking: At campsites only

Fee: None

Elevation: 15 feet

Restrictions

Pets—On 6-foot leash only

Fires—In fire rings only

Alcoholic beverages—At campsites only

Vehicles—None

CAYO COSTA CAMPGROUND

North Fort Myers

C ayo Costa is a barrier island that is accessible only by water. A trip here calls for a little planning, but it's more than worth it. If you like miles of unspoiled beaches, Gulf sunsets, and a tent-only campground, this is the place for you.

Your first step is to get a reservation on the ferry boat *Tropic Star*. Call (941) 283-0015 to reserve your seat. Then bring *everything* you will need for your camping trip. There are no stores on the island and no convenient access to one once you are on it. Then, get to the ferry on time and enjoy the 90-minute ride from Pine Island to Cayo Costa.

Once you get there, register for your campsite. Next, a park tram will take you from the bay side of the island to the Gulf side, where the campground is located. It's a little bothersome loading and unloading your gear on the boat and tram, but once you get set up, you'll wonder why you didn't get here sooner.

The tram drops you off at the campground. Resist the urge to run to the white beach and blue water; pick your campsite first. Follow the beachside sandy path running through a stand of Australian pines to a more open area of sea grape and other native plants. A hundred yards of sporadic sea oats divide you from the ocean. Campsites 1 through 3 are in the shade of the pines and look out on the Gulf.

The remaining nine campsites are sunny overhead but are separated by sea grapes.

CAMPGROUND RATINGS

Beauty:	★★★★★
Site privacy:	★★★
Site spaciousness:	★★★
Quiet:	★★★★★
Security:	★★★★★
Cleanliness/upkeep:	★★★★

Take a ferry to South Florida's best seaside tent camping.

The skeletons of dead Australian pines above you stand testimony to the park policy of eliminating these exotics. All of these sites feature an ocean view.

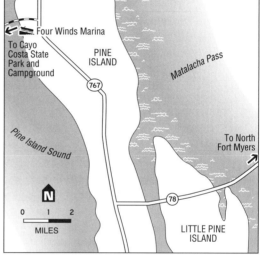

A spur path goes behind the small dune at campsite 5 and contains campsites 13 through 24. The sites are shielded from the wind, which make them a little buggier yet warm during infrequent cold spells. The beach vegetation, primarily sea grape and palm, provides adequate site privacy.

The other six campsites are on a path of their own, back from the beach beneath some Australian pines with some bigger thickets of sea grape. These sites are very shady, and look out on one another, though some of the sites are tucked away in the thickets of sea grape.

Three comfort stations serve the campground and some nearby cabins. Walk toward the cabins to the first comfort station. It has a shower, but it is in the open. This can be advantageous, when that afternoon sun warms you as the cold water runs down your back. The other comfort stations have enclosed showers for each sex on the outside of the building. All comfort stations have flush toilets and running sinks for each sex.

Winter is the time to come here. The sky is sunny, the breeze cool. The bugs are much less of a problem. It is not oppressively hot, as it can be in the summer. Bring bug repellent and a tent with fine mesh netting no matter what the season. Call ahead and ask about the insect conditions.

A sense of elation came over me as I got to the island. It was simply beautiful. Palm trees, live oaks, tall pines, and beach, beach, beach everywhere. I combed the beach first. Cayo Costa is known for its shelling. After storms, the beach is littered with all descriptions of shells. Next, I went for a swim. The Gulf waters here are clear and turquoise blue.

After my swim, I rented a bike at the Ranger Station to explore the island. There are five island trails. A bike is the perfect way to see the old pioneer cemetery and the dense oak-palm hammocks in the center of the island. Next, I pedaled to Quarantine Point and gazed out at the sailboats in the bay. An afternoon breeze kicked up as I pedaled on the Gulf Trail, which runs for nearly 3 miles within sight of the beach.

Sunbathers took in the rays. Some campers surf-fished for flounder, redfish, and snook. Others just strolled along the beach, enjoying the ocean breeze. Later that evening, I ate supper with some new friends I had met on the ferry. Then we all took one last walk to watch the sunset. As if the day hadn't been magical enough, a full moon rose, illuminating the sea in a thousand points of light, as gentle waves lapped the shore.

Remember this: On the day of your return to the mainland, the ferry doesn't leave Cayo Costa until 3 P.M. Plan accordingly. I used my morning and afternoon to walk the trails and to visit with my new friends. There is a sense of camaraderie here on Cayo Costa, like you're all shipwrecked together. I think everybody is extra friendly because they are so happy to be here. Come to Cayo Costa and you will have that feeling, too.

To get there from North Fort Meyers, take FL 78 for 16 miles to Pine Island. Turn right where 78 ends and go 4 miles to Four Winds Marina. It will be on your left. The *Tropic Star* will boat you out to Cayo Costa.

KEY INFORMATION

Cayo Costa Barrier Islands
P.O. Box 1150
Boca Grande, FL 33921

Operated by: Florida State Parks

Information: (941) 964-0375

Open: Year-round

Individual sites: 30

Each site has: Picnic table, fire grates

Site assignment: First come, first served; no reservations

Registration: At Ranger Station on island

Facilities: Cold showers, flush toilets, piped water

Parking: At Four Winds Marina on Pine Island

Fee: $14 per night

Elevation: Sea level

Restrictions

Pets—Prohibited

Fires—In fire grates only

Alcoholic beverages—Prohibited

Vehicles—Not allowed on island

Other—14-day stay limit

FLAMINGO CAMPGROUND

Homestead

Flamingo was once a fishing village, cut off from the rest of Florida by the sea of saw grass known as the Everglades, accessible only by boat. Since that time, the park service has built a scenic road to Flamingo, which passes several Everglades attractions on the way to Florida Bay. Once here, you can pitch your tent and go about the business of enjoying this unique ecosystem.

Flamingo Campground is very large. There are over 250 campsites in the entire campground. But the park service has kindly set aside a section for tent campers only. It has 64 campsites with an incredible ocean view. Being subdivided, the Flamingo feels like three separate campgrounds rather than one huge one. Campers prefer to be in Flamingo because it harbors the oceanic characteristics of the Everglades.

The main campground begins behind the registration booth. There are four loops. One loop is actually for trailers only; the other three are for RV and tent campers. Stay in the latter three loops if you must, but it is unlikely that the tent-only area will be full. The loop area has a smattering of palms and mahogany trees to break up the grassy understory.

Turn left beyond the registration booth to the walk-in tent area. Park your vehicle in the spaces provided for tent campers. The tenters' area lies between you and Florida Bay. The campsites are arranged by num-

CAMPGROUND RATINGS

Beauty:	★★★★
Site privacy:	★
Site spaciousness:	★★★★★
Quiet:	★★
Security:	★★★
Cleanliness/upkeep:	★★★

Take a short walk to your campsite right on Florida Bay in Everglades National Park.

bered sites in a somewhat
hodgepodge fashion in a large
grassy field, some 200 yards
wide and 100 yards deep.

There is a complete lack of
privacy between sites, except
for the sheer distances of the
campground. The campsites
are placed well away from one
another, with more room than
you will need, especially since
you carry your gear from car
to campsite.

Fourteen campsites are
directly on Florida Bay. A few
trees lie on the oceanfront.
These campsites overlook the

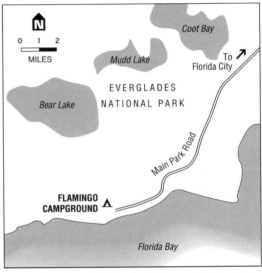

small mangrove-covered keys dotting the bay. These small keys derive their
name from the Spanish word *cayo*, meaning "island." The ocean views continu-
ally change with the time of day. But never, ever are they less than spectacular.

I was initially disappointed upon seeing the layout of this campground. But
after getting acclimated to the openness of sky, field, and sea, I came to appreciate its unusual nature. The ocean breeze was welcome. Fellow tent campers
I met shared stories of their experiences in the Everglades.

Two comfort stations service this campground. One provides cold-water
showers and flush toilets; the other has flush toilets only. The park service
maintains a close eye for campers trying to sneak onto the field without pay-
ing, so be prepared to show your receipt.

Flamingo is best enjoyed during the winter season. Summer can be very
rainy and very buggy. No matter when you come, bring a tent with adequate
ventilation and netting. Bring long sleeves and long pants. Don't forget the
bug dope!

Once settled in, walk to the Flamingo Visitor Center to get oriented. There
are many ranger-led orientation programs. The ecosystem of the Everglades

is an interesting story indeed. Sign up for a boat tour at the marina. Rent a motorboat and try your luck with rod and reel. Canoes and bicycles are available for rent there as well. Guided hikes and canoe trips are scheduled for the area. Check the local activity boards for your best bet.

If you like to discover the natural world on your own, there are ample opportunities. Hikers have eight excellent hikes from which to choose. Snake Bight, Christian Point, and the Coastal Prairie trails are my favorites. Snake Bight exudes that tropical look and ends at a bird-watcher's boardwalk. Christian Point travels through multiple Everglades habitats. The Coastal Prairie Trail follows an old fishermen's path toward the unspoiled beaches of Cape Sable. Check at the Visitor Center for trailheads and directions.

Canoeists have seven trails to paddle in the immediate area. See alligators and crocodiles on the West Lake Trail. Paddle the narrow passageways of the Noble Hammock Trail. The Nine Mile Pond Trail makes a 5-mile loop through saw grass and mangroves. Canoes are already waiting at the beginning of these trails, making rental easy. Again, inquire at the Visitor Center.

Flamingo can be anything you make it. Pick your campsite and jump into any of the activities that suit your fancy. Just make it back in time for sunset over Florida Bay.

To get there from U.S. 1 in Florida City, follow the signs south to Everglades National Park. Flamingo Campground is 38 miles beyond the park entrance gate on the main campground road.

KEY INFORMATION

Flamingo Campground
P.O. Box 279
Homestead, FL 33030

Operated by: Everglades National Park

Information: (305) 242-7700

Open: Year-round

Individual sites: 64 tent only

Each site has: Tent area, stand-up fire grill

Site assignment: First come, first served; no reservations

Registration: At registration booth, or call (800) 365-CAMP

Facilities: Cold showers, flush toilet, water spigot

Parking: At walk-in site parking lot

Fee: $14 per night

Elevation: Sea level

Restrictions

Pets—On 6-foot leash at all times

Fires—In grills only

Alcoholic beverages—At campsites only

Vehicles—None

Other—14 days total from November to April; 30-day stay limit in calendar year

SOUTH FLORIDA

HIGHLANDS HAMMOCK CAMPGROUND

Sebring

Don't think that wilderness preserva-tion is some new concept invented shortly after the first Earth Day. Highlands Hammock is proof that preservation has been around awhile. When south-central Florida's forests began to fall to the axe for citrus cultivation, some folks in the area decided that this particular forest was too long in natural development to be cut down for a buck.

Just about that time, the Great Depres-sion came along. The land was bought and the Civilian Conservation Corps was put to work, making this state park user-friendly. Not too much improvement is necessary, though, when you already have brooding cypress swamps, wild orange trees, and thousand-year-old live oaks. To top it off, a settler from the early days cleared a plot in the center of the park, preserving a little human history in this scenic swath of the Sunshine State.

Highlands Hammock is a popular winter park. Since the addition of the primitive campground, it is on my must-see list for those who want to see the real Florida.

The main campground consists of 138 campsites. There are five loops all of which spur off the main campground road. The campground is in a shaded forest of live oak, with a smattering of pine. The palmet-to understory is adequate for site privacy.

Twenty-five sites in the main campground don't have electricity and lie along a gravel

CAMPGROUND RATINGS

Beauty: ★★★★
Site privacy: ★★★
Site spaciousness: ★★★★★
Quiet: ★★★
Security: ★★★
Cleanliness/upkeep: ★★★

The primitive campground and lush nature trails make one of Florida's original state parks a winner.

road. It is mainly pine woods here. Stay in these campsites if you must stay in the main campground. Four bathhouses serve the whole area.

The primitive campground is located on a spur road of its own. Turn left beyond the park entrance booth onto a somewhat rough sand road. This road passes a few potholes on its mile-long journey to the primitive campground, eliminating all RVs and making this area a de facto tent-only campground.

The first seven sites start on the right of the road in an open pine forest, with small live oaks and clumps of palmetto. Each site is big enough for five tents. Grass grows all around the sites. Pass the portable toilet and come to the next set of campsites. The woods are a bit thicker here. The undergrowth is lusher as well.

The last four campsites are beneath a mature live oak and pine forest. These are the best sites. Campsite 16, is the only site on the left-hand side of the road. It also happens to be the best and most private site in the park. By all means, stay in the primitive area if you can. Then come to the main campground to take a shower and get your water. It's OK with the park staff.

A camping area wouldn't be here if not for the scenic old-growth woodlands of Highlands Hammock. No less than five indigenous Florida plant communities thrive here. A 3.2-mile loop road winds through these communities. The road is popular for autos and bicycles and doubles as a fitness trail. The ranger-led tram ride takes campers on a guided tour of the forest along this road. This road may sound crowded, but it's not.

The best way to see these special lands is by foot. There are eight separate nature trails that wind through the park. Some of these are interconnected. I walked them all and enjoyed every minute of it. The Cypress Swamp Trail travels a boardwalk through a wet, primeval world of alligators, fish, and birds.

The Ancient Hammock Trail travels through a mature hardwood forest, where the tree canopy is made of southern hardwoods and the understory is very tropical and includes wild orange trees. Hike the Young Hammock Trail to see how a pine forest evolves into hardwood. My favorite trail is the Big Oak Trail. I marveled at the sight of gnarled and worn live oaks that have stood for a millennium!

Another must-do is to get a wild orange shake from Baileys Camp Store. While you are there, go across the veranda to the Civilian Conservation Corps Museum and learn the story of those who made this park a reality. Bikers have another 6 miles of dirt paths to follow on the Off-Road Bike Trail. Bicycles are for rent at the Ranger Station. Walkers are welcome on this trail, too.

If somehow you find yourself bored, then go to the Ranger Station where you'll find humorous list of the top 25 things to do at Highlands Hammock State Park. That should keep you busy.

To get there from U.S. 27 in Sebring, turn onto FL 634 and follow it 4 miles to Highlands Hammock State Park.

KEY INFORMATION

Highlands Hammock Campground
5931 Hammock Road
Sebring, FL 33872

Operated by: Florida State Parks

Information: (941) 386-6094

Open: Year-round

Individual sites: 138 at main campground, 16 primitive

Each site has: Main campground: picnic table, fire grill, water, electricity; primitive: picnic table, fire grate

Site assignment: Assigned by ranger unless specific site asked for

Registration: By phone or at park entrance booth

Facilities: Hot showers, flush toilets, pay phone, laundry

Parking: At campsites only

Fee: $13 per night December to March, $8 per night April to November; $2 electricity fee

Elevation: 80 feet

Restrictions

  Pets—Prohibited

  Fires—In fire grates only

  Alcoholic beverages—Prohibited

  Vehicles—None

  Other—14-day stay limit

JOHN PENNEKAMP CAMPGROUND

Key Largo

This park protects part of the only living coral reef in the United States. The powers that be have made exploring this coral reef easy for everyone. Beware: The campground is nowhere near as enticing as the rest of the park, but you would never know it by the efforts you have to put forth to get a campsite here.

Just as the other state parks in the Keys, you are better off reserving a campsite 60 days in advance of your arrival. But once here, the campsite is yours for up to 14 days, as long as you renew it every day. And judging by the prices of the other campgrounds in the area, John Pennekamp is a bargain. You will still have to put up with some RVs. But since electricity is provided for each site, generator noise won't be a problem.

The campground forms a **U** around a tidal creek and pond. The sites are neither very big nor overly attractive. There are adequate shade trees at the campsites, but vegetation buffers between the sites are few. So don't jump naked out of your tent in the morning if this is your normal camping routine.

Campsites 1 through 22 abut the creek and pond. They generally have less vegetation than the sites on the other side of the campground. Campsites 23 through 40 run parallel to sites 1 through 22. They are backed against a thick stand of woods. Some of these have an adequate vegetation

CAMPGROUND RATINGS

Beauty:	★★★
Site privacy:	★★
Site spaciousness:	★★
Quiet:	★★
Security:	★★★★
Cleanliness/upkeep:	★★★

There are several ways to enjoy this spectacular undersea park, the first in the United States.

buffer offering a little more privacy. The final six sites follow the **U** back to the front of the campground.

Complete bathhouses are found at either end of the compact campground, affording easy access for all. This campground is not the greatest, but it will serve any tent camper who wants to check out what this state park has to offer.

Nearly 180 undersea nautical square miles are growing and waiting for you. The clear, warm waters are alive with fish, turtles, lobsters, and plant

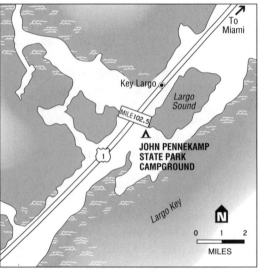

life. Have you ever wanted to dive? There is an on-site dive shop that offers open-water certification for the novice and advanced open-water certification for those who already know a thing or two about tanks and such. If that sounds a little too much, go snorkeling. It's easy with on-site equipment rental and guided tours of the reef. And if you would like to see the coral reef but don't want to get wet, go on the glass-bottom boat tour.

Boat lovers can rent fishing boats, canoes, sea cycles, and sailboats. All of these are ready to go at the marina in the center of the park. A 2.5-mile marked canoe trail winds through the park's mangrove wilderness. Maybe you want to see a fish at the end of your rod instead of on the coral reef. There are plenty here at John Pennekamp.

Sunbathers have two beaches to choose from. Far Beach is at the less-crowded, east end of the park. Cannon Beach is larger. It is by the main concession area. A roped-off swimming area makes it safer for families. A replica of an old Spanish galleon is located 130 feet off the shore of this beach.

Landlubbers can check out the two nature trails. Step from the marina parking area onto the Wild Tamarind Trail and enter the forest that once covered much of the Keys. Visually, it's very stimulating; however, you can't escape the sounds of U.S. 1. I enjoyed it nonetheless. Because without this state park, even this small woodland would be a T-shirt shop.

Hike the Mangrove Trail. It is the only way you will ever get in the middle of a mangrove thicket without sinking up to your thighs in muck. That's because you follow a boardwalk that has interpretive signs along the way to help you appreciate how a mangrove stand functions. I always enjoy these little trails. It helps me understand how every place is unique and is just one more strand in the intricate web of nature.

The natural features of John Pennekamp make up for the fair campground. Don't pass this place by. And with all there is to do here, you will be too tired to care if it is not the world's finest place to set up a tent.

To get there, look for John Pennekamp at mile marker 102.5 on U.S. 1.

KEY INFORMATION

John Pennekamp Campground
P.O. Box 1560
Key Largo, FL 33037

Operated by: Florida State Parks

Information: (305) 451-1202

Open: Year-round

Individual sites: 46

Each site has: Tent pad, picnic table, fire grill, water, electricity

Site assignment: First come, first served; assigned if reservations made

Registration: 23 sites for phone registration only, 23 sites for on-site registration

Facilities: Hot showers, flush toilets, pay phone

Parking: At campsites only

Fee: $24 per night; $2 electricity fee

Elevation: Sea level

Restrictions

Pets—Prohibited

Fires—In fire grates only

Alcoholic beverages—Prohibited

Vehicles—None

Other—14-day stay limit

SOUTH FLORIDA

JONATHAN DICKINSON CAMPGROUND

Hobe Sound

Jonathan Dickinson stumbled on this area when he was shipwrecked in the late 1600s. You need only drive here to see what the southeast coast of Florida looked like before the massive development of today. There are two quality campgrounds from which to choose and a host of sights and activities to select from, too.

Near the park entrance is the Pine Grove Camping Area. It is laid out in a grid form, like city streets, beneath a dense canopy of nonnative Australian pines. These trees lend nearly complete shade to the campground. Their highly acidic needles inhibit growth of other plants once they fall to the ground. And the ground here is covered with the needles. The trees are slowly being removed and replaced with native plants, though not without protest from campers who enjoy the cool shade beneath their heights.

Two comfort stations are located here. One is in the center of the camping grid and the other is on the south end of the camping area. The sites on the outside of the grid are more open and sunny. Site spaciousness is not a problem anywhere. The campsites in the center of the grid have a thick enough understory for more than adequate site privacy.

The River Camping Area is near the remarkable Loxahatchie River, though no campsites are directly riverside. The River Camping Area houses the 45 campsites

CAMPGROUND RATINGS

Beauty:	★★★
Site privacy:	★★★
Site spaciousness:	★★★
Quiet:	★★★
Security:	★★★★
Cleanliness/upkeep:	★★★

A globally imperiled forest and Florida's only nationally designated wild and scenic river, combined with two great campgrounds, make Jonathan Dickinson a special state park.

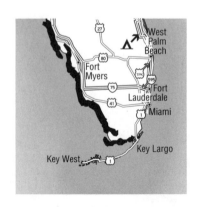

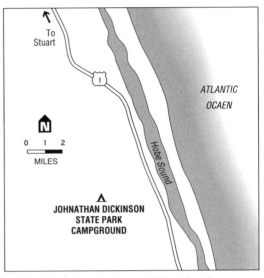

using the standard loop design, though most of the campsites are on the inside of the loop. Slash pines tower over the camping area. A heavy understory of palmetto divides the campsites, which are covered with well-maintained St. Augustine grass.

The buffers of palmetto provide maximum site privacy, but their overgrowth compromises site spaciousness in comparison with the Pine Grove Camping Area. A lone comfort station in the center of the loop serves the campground. This camping area is my favorite of the two. The flora is the real Florida, the campsite buffers are superior, and I like my sites a little more open. Both will serve tent campers well.

After choosing your campground, what do you do? Start by learning more about the coastal sand pine scrub forest. It covers 20% of the park's 11,500 acres. This forest once covered much of the southeast coast of Florida. Now it is so rare that it is listed as a "globally imperiled" ecosystem.

Go directly to the Hobe Mountain observation tower. Mountains in Florida, you say? Here, the "mountains" are sandy hills that are cloaked in the fast-disappearing plant community. It is a 20-minute walk up the sandy trail to the tower. Look over the Atlantic Ocean and the south of Florida. Natural views like this are unusual in the Sunshine State.

For a change of pace, check out the superlatively beautiful Loxahatchee River. There are two ways to do this. Self-motivators can rent a canoe and see for themselves the hardwood forest and cypress trees along the river. Keep your eyes peeled for alligators or a stray manatee. Or you can take the boat tour of the river aboard the Loxahatchee Queen II. It offers a two-hour trip with an informative guide who will tell all the secrets of the river. It is hard to believe this park has two such different, yet special, ecosystems so close together.

No matter how you get there, make sure to end up at Trapper Nelson's Place on the Loxahatchee River. It is only accessible by boat. Here you can learn about the man who came to this area to hunt and trap, earning the moniker "Wildman of the Loxahatchee." Explore his cabin and grounds and where he built his own wildlife zoo.

There are other things to do here as well. Bikers can pedal the park roads or enjoy their own special trail. Anglers can cast a line for both saltwater and freshwater species of fish. A section of the Florida National Scenic Trail winds through the coastal sand pine scrub forest. Use the East Loop Trail to bring you back to your starting point near the park entrance. The Kitching Creek Trail features a one-hour walk that explores yet more of this sizable state park.

The diversity of habitat and two campgrounds give you plenty of choices at Jonathan Dickinson State Park. First, make the choice to come here. But there is no need to wreck your ship to land in this piece of valuable Florida real estate.

To get there from Stuart, drive south on U.S. 1 for 12 miles. Jonathan Dickinson State Park will be on your right.

KEY INFORMATION

Jonathan Dickinson Campground
16450 S.E. Federal Highway
Hobe Sound, FL 33455

Operated by: Florida State Parks

Information: (407) 546-2771

Open: Year-round

Individual sites: 135

Each site has: Tent pad, picnic table, fire grill, water, electricity

Site assignment: Assigned by ranger unless specific site asked for

Registration: By phone or at park entrance booth

Facilities: Hot showers, flush toilets, pay phone, soda machine

Parking: At campsites and extra car parking area

Fee: $14 per night May to November, $17 per night December to April

Elevation: 20 feet

Restrictions

Pets—Prohibited

Fires—In fire grates only

Alcoholic beverages—Prohibited

Vehicles—None

Other—14-day stay limit

LONG KEY CAMPGROUND

Long Key

Look out from your campsite. Teal-blue waters extend as far as the eye can see. A small beach is the only thing between you and your campsite, nestled in tropical woods. The lovely waters of the Florida Keys are your playground here at Long Key State Recreation Area.

There is very little undeveloped land left in the Keys. Long Key State Recreation Area is just a sliver of the real Florida on a sliver of an island. But the 883 acres of "nonsubmergible" land packs a powerful punch. Of course, you'll want to explore the submergible land, especially that part with ocean above it.

Winter is Long Key's busy time. Make reservations if you know when you are coming. Do it exactly 60 days before your planned arrival. And call at 8 A.M. Remember, you are guaranteed a campsite only for as many days as you have paid for. And, while we're discussing the downside, U.S. 1 runs a little close to the campground. Unfortunately, in the land-starved Keys, everything is packed tight.

Pass the entrance gate and turn right. The campground is to your left, between you and the Atlantic Ocean. All 60 sites run perpendicular to the ocean. Each campsite has its own oceanfront footage. Between each campsite is a vegetation buffer. And as the park's buffer restoration project continues, the buffers will become even thicker than they are today,

CAMPGROUND RATINGS

Beauty:	★★★★★
Site privacy:	★★★
Site spaciousness:	★★★
Quiet:	★
Security:	★★★
Cleanliness/upkeep:	★★★

*Every campsite at Long Key
has an ocean view.*

which is adequately thick for site privacy.

Larger trees appear as the campsites run westerly. Sites 1 through 10 have shorter vegetation. By the time you get to campsite 20, the tropical forest is in full glory. Thankfully, the wooded buffer across from the campground shields some of the auto noise of U.S. 1.

But don't let the traffic noise get to you; this campground is simply too scenic. And the ocean views—from your tent, from your picnic table, while you cook or read a magazine—

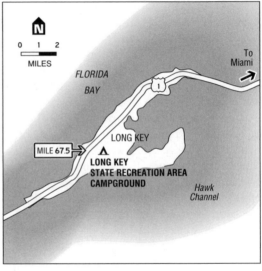

they are what you imagine as you dream of those warm sunny days and breezy Keys nights. Listen to the waves lap against the shoreline.

Six water spigots are located in the campground. But they are all located along the first 30 sites. So, if you stay at sites 30 through 60, grab your water by the bucketful. The three bathhouses are evenly spread throughout the campground. A single dump station with recycling bins serves all campers.

A primitive camping area with six sites is located in the old picnic shelters by the Golden Orb Trail. Theses are located in a mangrove thicket, have little or no breeze and "can be very buggy," according to one park ranger. Furthermore, you have to tote your gear over a boardwalk to the shelter. But the campsites are cheap.

We arrived at Long Key on a rainy day. We set up a tarp and cooked stir-fry shrimp obtained at a local fish market. The rain and the big meal lulled us into a nap. The rain had quit when we awoke, so we decided to explore Long Key.

First we hiked the hour-long Golden Orb Trail; it winds along the shoreline. You can see the Gulf Stream flowing 4 miles out at sea. Close views include mangrove thickets and salt-intolerant hardwood hammocks that grow only at the highest points in the Keys. Steam rose from the sand in the open woods away from the beach.

Next, we grabbed the canoe and paddled the Long Key Lakes Canoe Trail. It starts near the park entrance. We followed the numbered posts, learning more about tidal lagoons, the "nurseries of the sea." These tidal lagoons are the beginning of the ocean food chain for creatures of the sea and for birds as well. The clouds broke and a rainbow appeared. It was a good sign.

Another trail at Long Key is the Lathon Trail. This one is for hikers, though. It starts across U.S. 1 and explores the tropical forest and shoreline of the Gulf side of Long Key. There is a fine swimming beach adjacent to the picnic area.

Other activities are centered around the beautiful Gulf waters. Flats fishing or deep-water fishing, snorkeling, and shelling keep campers busy. We watched a fantastic Keys sunset and kicked back at our campsite, just taking in the breeze. After you get your campsite, you have nothing left to worry about in this laid-back campground.

To get there, look for Long Key State Recreation Area at mile marker 67.5 on U.S. 1.

KEY INFORMATION

Long Key Campground
P.O. Box 776
Long Key, FL 33001

Operated by: Florida State Parks

Information: (305) 664-4815

Open: Year-round

Individual sites: 66

Each site has: Tent pad, picnic table, fire grill, ocean view

Site assignment: First come, first served; assigned if reservations made

Registration: 30 sites for phone registration only; 36 sites for on-site registration

Facilities: Hot showers, flush toilets, water spigots

Parking: At campsites only

Fee: Main campground $24 per site; primitive sites $5.50 per person

Elevation: Sea level

Restrictions

Pets—Prohibited

Fires—In grills only

Alcoholic beverages—Prohibited

Vehicles—None

Other—14-day stay limit

LONG PINE KEY CAMPGROUND

Homestead

Set in a forest of fragrant southern slash pine, Long Pine Key Campground has a pace as slow as the waters that flow through the river of saw grass that is the Everglades. But the Everglades are not all saw grass. Another important plant community of this park is the pine flatwoods. These pines grow on limestone that was once an ancient coral reef.

The campground is part of an area known as the Pinelands. The 107 campsites stretch around one side of a quiet lake. A picnic area lies on the other side. The campsites are situated on an elongated loop with crossroads that connect one side of the loop to the other. There are 11 crossroads that split the loop.

Most of the campsites are along these 11 crossroads. The campsites are very spacious and are divided by the understory of the pine flatwoods, primarily saw palmetto and hardwood seedlings. These hardwood seedlings would grow and alter the forest from pine to hardwood, but lightning-caused fires destroy the undergrowth and the mature pines' tough bark is able to withstand the periodic fires.

The lakeview campsites are the most desirable. By the way, swimming is not allowed in the lake. I assume it is because of alligators. The campground is rarely full, save for the winter holidays. Winter is the busiest, most pleasant time to be here. It is the dry season in the Everglades, and

CAMPGROUND RATINGS

Beauty:	★★★★
Site privacy:	★★★
Site spaciousness:	★★★★★
Quiet:	★★
Security:	★★★
Cleanliness/upkeep:	★★★★

Stay in relaxed and secluded Long Pine Key, where you are near many Everglades highlights.

the bug population is minimal. But there will be some "snow-birds" at Big Pine Key in their RVs, escaping the chill of the North.

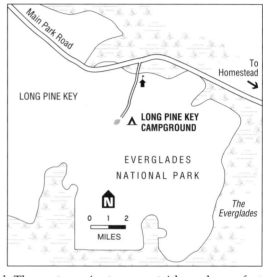

I stayed at one of the sites on the outside of the loop facing the piney woods. Like the other sites here, mine offered a grassy, mowed lawn, with the maximum in spaciousness and an acceptable amount of privacy. I enjoyed looking over the tall pines, smelling their distinct odor while gathering firewood.

Three clean comfort stations serve the well-kept campground. The water spigots are outside each comfort station. There is also a large washbasin at each comfort station. A campground host mans the entrance for your safety. The only things you should be wary of are the raccoons. Store your food properly or these critters will get your groceries when you leave. And leave you must, to explore the one and only Everglades.

Road-weary campers need only step away from the campground to see the Pinelands. A set of interconnecting trails emanates from Long Pine Key. The backbone of the trail system is the 6.7-mile Long Pine Key Nature Trail. It winds through the pine flatwoods, saw grass prairie, and hardwood hammocks, ending near Pine Glades Lake.

These hardwood hammocks are islands of tropical plant life, with wild palms, mahogany trees and live oaks. There are nearly 20 miles of trails to tramp in the immediate area of the campground. Get a trail map at the registration booth and make your own loop.

Just a short drive away at the Royal Palm Visitor Center are two of the park's premier interpretive footpaths, Gumbo Limbo and Anhinga Trails. The

Gumbo Limbo Trail leads through a hardwood hammock that features flora of the West Indies, such as gumbo limbo, royal palm, ferns and vines, which all lend a junglelike atmosphere. The Anhinga Trail is a scenic boardwalk on the sea of saw grass leading to Taylor Slough, a wildlife photographer's paradise. A plethora of birds, alligators, and other creatures dwell in this piece of the Everglades.

Auto tourists can drive to the Pa-hay-okee Overlook, west of Long Pine Key. Climb the observation tower and look around. The sky, the saw grass and the hardwood hammocks extend to the horizon. We drove here for a most dramatic sunrise. A few miles west on the main road is Mahogany Hammock. It contains the largest mahogany tree in America, as well as a menagerie of unusual flora and fauna.

No matter where you go in the Everglades, don't rush yourself. Stop, look, listen. This is a unique ecosystem, unlike any other on our planet. Its beauty is expansive and subtle, intricate and fragile. Here, life proceeds at its own pace. Leave the hurried world behind, make Long Pine Key your base camp, and get on Everglades time.

To get there from U.S. 1 in Homestead, follow the signs south along CR 9336 to Everglades National Park. Stay on the main park road. The signed turn to Long Pine Key is 6 miles beyond the park Visitor Center. Turn left and drive 0.5 mile to the campground.

KEY INFORMATION

Long Pine Key
P.O. Box 279
Homestead, FL 33030

Operated by: Everglades National Park

Information: (305) 242-7700

Open: Year-round

Individual sites: 107

Each site has: Picnic table, fire pit

Site assignment: Assigned by campground manager unless specific site is asked for

Registration: At campground registration booth, or call (800) 365-CAMP

Facilities: Flush toilets, water spigots

Parking: At campsites only

Fee: $14 per night

Elevation: 4 feet

Restrictions

Pets—On 6-foot leash only

Fires—In fire pits only

Alcoholic beverages—At campsites only

Vehicles—None

Other—14 days total from November to April; 30-day stay limit in calendar year

OSCAR SCHERER CAMPGROUND

Osprey

When you combine the outdoor features of Myakka River, Oscar Scherer, and Casey Key, you get a full plate of southwest Florida landscape with enough activities to wear you out daily. The campground of Oscar Scherer is the area's best, offering creekside campsites and ample privacy.

South Creek flows lazily through Oscar Scherer's 1,384 acres. Cross South Creek on a small bridge to access the campground. The campground is stretched out along South Creek's shaded bank, forming a narrow loop divided by four access roads.

Turn left after crossing the bridge. Sixteen creekside sites are on your left. Dense undergrowth keeps each site private. Tenters will favor these shaded sites. After you pass a footbridge, there is a spur road with four secluded creekside campsites.

Fourteen campsites lie away from the creek as the loop doubles back. These sites have privacy-yielding undergrowth, though shade trees are fewer than the creekside sites. Past the campfire circle are 26 more sites having the same buffer vegetation of the scrubby flatwoods.

Six drive-through sites are for RVs only as the loop doubles back again to border South Creek. Again, overhead shade becomes abundant. The final 31 creekside sites are among the first to go when this campground fills. Little footpaths course

CAMPGROUND RATINGS

Beauty: ★★★
Site privacy: ★★★
Site spaciousness: ★★★
Quiet: ★★
Security: ★★★★
Cleanliness/upkeep: ★★★★

Camp here and discover both Oscar Scherer and Myakka River State Parks.

---

throughout the woods to five bathhouses conveniently dispersed in the narrow loop's center. Each bathhouse has a hot shower for each sex.

This campground may sound large, but so much vegetation has been left intact. Campers can see only a few other sites other than their own, making it seem more intimate. Expect a few RVs, but electrical hookups at each site mean no generators to keep you awake. The busy season is from November through April. Getting reservations will ease your mind, but you will most likely get a site if you just show up.

Once you get a site, you probably won't be there too much. South Creek has canoeing and saltwater-fishing opportunities. Canoes can be rented at the Ranger Station. Two short nature trails, the Old Fisherman's Trail and South Creek Trail, run along the creek across from the campground. Lake Osprey, a freshwater lake, is a great place for swimming.

Oscar Scherer is home to two threatened plant communities, pine flatwoods and scrubby flatwoods. This high, dry, easily developed land is being cut down all over the state. But this protected tract has over 15 miles of interconnected trail for you to hike. The trails are generally easy and level. The White Trail is of particular note, circling South Creek as it flows out of the north. We are lucky Oscar Scherer donated this diminishing landscape for us to enjoy.

Nearby Myakka River State Park contains over 28,000 acres of the real Florida. It has unique plant and animal communities, too. By the way, the campground at Myakka River is cramped, open, and has too many RVs for me. But a trip here is worth the half-hour drive from Oscar Scherer. Why? Prairies, rivers, lakes, trails, and wildlife.

The Myakka River is the park's centerpiece. The river flows through the park and widens to become Upper Myakka Lake. Both bodies of water are suitable for canoeing and fishing. If you like tours, there is an airboat tour of the lake and a tram tour covering part of the park's 45 square miles.

The adventurous may want to explore the backcountry. Foot trails lace the park, passing oak hammocks, numerous ponds, and Florida's prairie lands. These prairies are remnants of 300,000 acres of prairie land that once covered the state's interior. Grasses, wildflowers, and palmetto cover this unique ecosystem that was kept open by lightning-induced fires.

Alligators are plentiful in this park and can be viewed during winter months. Deer, bobcats, and other wildlife are also plentiful. Myakka River also hosts a large population of birds, and the lakeside boardwalk is a great start for birders.

After you have exhausted yourself, hit the beach. It is just a short drive down U.S. 41 to the public beach on Casey Key. Here, you can relax by the beautiful Gulf waters and white sands. Then you will have enjoyed a full taste of Florida's southwest, with Oscar Scherer as your headquarters.

To get there, Oscar Scherer State Park is just south of Osprey on U.S. 41.

KEY INFORMATION

Oscar Scherer Campground
1843 South Tamiami Trail
Osprey, FL 34229

Operated by: Florida State Parks

Information: (941) 483-5956

Open: Year-round

Individual sites: 100

Each site has: Tent pad, picnic table, fire ring, water, electricity

Site assignment: First come, first served; assigned if reservations made

Registration: 50 sites for phone registration; 50 sites for on-site ranger registration

Facilities: Hot showers, flush toilets, pay phone

Parking: At campsites and in extra car parking areas

Fee: $16 per night; $2 electricity fee

Elevation: 5 feet

Restrictions

Pets—Prohibited

Fires—In fire rings only

Alcoholic beverages—Prohibited

Vehicles—None

Other—14-day stay limit

APPENDICES

APPENDIX A
Camping Equipment Checklist

Except for the large and bulky items on this list, I keep a plastic storage container full of the essentials of car camping so that they're ready to go when I am. I make a last-minute check of the inventory, resupply anything that's low or missing, and away I go!

Cooking Utensils
Bottle opener
Bottles of salt, pepper, spices, sugar,
    cooking oil, and maple syrup in
    waterproof, spillproof containers
Can opener
Cups, plastic or tin
Dish soap (biodegradable), sponge,
    and towel
Flatware
Food of your choice
Frying pan
Fuel for stove
Matches in waterproof container
Plates
Pocketknife
Pot with lid
Spatula
Stove
Tin foil
Wooden spoon

First Aid Kit
Band-Aids
First aid cream
Gauze pads
Ibuprofen or aspirin
Insect repellent
Moleskin
Snakebite kit
Sunscreen/Chap Stick
Tape, waterproof adhesive

Sleeping Gear
Pillow
Sleeping bag
Sleeping pad, inflatable or insulated
Tent with ground tarp and rainfly

Miscellaneous
Bath soap (biodegradable), washcloth,
    and towel
Camp chair
Candles
Cooler
Deck of cards
Fire starter
Flashlight with fresh batteries
Foul-weather clothing
Lantern
Maps (road, topographic, trails, etc.)
Paper towels
Plastic zip-top bags
Sunglasses
Toilet paper
Water bottle
Wool blanket

Optional
Barbecue grill
Binoculars
Field guides on bird, plant, and
    wildlife identification
Fishing rod and tackle
Hatchet

APPENDIX B
Information

Appalachicola National Forest
Woodcrest Office Park
325 John Knox Road
Suite F-100
Tallahassee, FL 32303
(904) 942-9300

Florida Division of Tourism
Collins Building
107 West Gaines Street
Tallahassee, FL 32301
(904) 487-1462

Florida State Forests
3125 Conner Boulevard
Tallahassee, FL 32399-1650
(904) 488-6611

Florida State Parks
3900 Commonwealth Boulevard
Mail Station 500
Tallahassee, FL 32399-3000
(904) 488-6131

Ocala National Forest
10863 East Highway 40
Silver Springs, FL 34488
(352) 625-2520

Osceola National Forest
U.S. Highway 90
P.O. Box 70
Olustee, FL 32072
(904) 752-2577

National Park System Areas in Florida
National Park Service
Southeast Field Area
75 Spring Street, SW
Atlanta, GA 30303
(404) 331-4290

APPENDIX C
S u g g e s t e d   R e a d i n g   a n d   R e f e r e n c e

A Canoe and Kayaking Guide to the Streams of Florida, Volume I, North Central Peninsula and Panhandle. Carter, Elizabeth & John L. Pearce. Menasha Ridge Press, 1985.

A Canoe and Kayaking Guide to the Streams of Florida, Volume II, Central and South Peninsula. Glaros, Lou & Doug Sphar. Menasha Ridge Press, 1987.

The Hikers Guide to Florida. O'Keefe, Timothy. Falcon Press, 1990.

A Hiking Guide to the Trails of Florida. Carter, Elizabeth. Menasha Ridge Press, 1987.

A Visitors Guide to the Everglades. Weber, Jeff. Florida Flair Books, 1994.

The Everglades: River of Grass. Douglas, Marjorie Stoneman. Mockingbird Books, 1947.

Great Adventures in Florida. O'Keefe, Timothy. Menasha Ridge Press, 1996.

Mountain Bike! Florida; A Guide to the Classic Trails. Jones, Steve. Menasha Ridge Press, 1997.

ABOUT THE AUTHOR

A native Tennessean, Johnny Molloy was born in Memphis and moved to Knoxville in 1980 to attend the University of Tennessee. It was there, on a backpacking foray into the Great Smoky Mountains National Park (GSMNP), that he developed a love of the natural world—a love that has become the primary focus of his life.

Though a disaster, that trip unleashed a passion for the outdoors that has encompassed more than 1,200 nights in the wild over the past 12 years. He has spent over 650 nights in the Smokies alone, cultivating his woodmanship and expertise on those lofty mountains. He has completed his fourth year as a GSMNP adopt-a-trail volunteer and currently maintains Little Bottoms Trail.

After graduating from the University of Tennessee in 1987 and continuing to spend ever-increasing time in natural places, he became more skilled in a variety of environments. Upon suggestion and encouragement from friends, he began to parlay his skill into an occupation. The results of his efforts are three books: *Day & Overnight Hikes in the Great Smoky Mountains National Park* (Menasha Ridge Press, 1995); *Trial by Trail: Backpacking in the Smoky Mountains* (University of Tennessee Press, 1996); and *The Best in Tent Camping: Smoky Mountains* (Menasha Ridge Press, 1997). In addition, he has authored numerous magazine articles.

Today, Johnny continues to write about, and travel extensively to, all four corners of the United States indulging in a variety of outdoor pursuits. He has recently completed a book about a summer in the West entitled *West by Southeast*, as well as another book for Menasha Ridge Press entitled *Day & Overnight Hikes in the Shenandoah National Park*.